Puffin Books

AF746512

Help Around the House

Morris Gleitzman grew up in England and came to Australia when he was sixteen. After university he worked for ten years as a screenwriter. Then he had a wonderful experience. He wrote a novel for young people. Now, after 40 books, he's one of Australia's most popular authors. He was appointed the Australian Children's Laureate for 2018–2019.

Visit Morris at his website:
morrisgleitzman.com

Books by Morris Gleitzman

The Other Facts of Life
Second Childhood
Two Weeks with the Queen
Misery Guts
Worry Warts
Puppy Fat
Blabber Mouth
Sticky Beak
Gift of the Gab
Belly Flop
Water Wings
Wicked! (with Paul Jennings)
Deadly! (with Paul Jennings)
Bumface
Adults Only
Teacher's Pet
Toad Rage
Toad Heaven
Toad Away
Toad Surprise
Toad Delight
Boy Overboard
Girl Underground
Worm Story
Aristotle's Nostril
Doubting Thomas
Grace
Too Small to Fail
Extra Time
Loyal Creatures
Help Around the House
Give Peas a Chance
Pizza Cake
Snot Chocolate
Funny Stories
Once
Then
After
Soon
Now
Maybe

MORRIS GLEITZMAN

Help Around the House

Puffin Books

PUFFIN BOOKS

UK | USA | Canada | Ireland | Australia
India | New Zealand | South Africa | China

Penguin Books is part of the Penguin Random House group of companies
whose addresses can be found at global.penguinrandomhouse.com.

Penguin Random House Australia

First published by Penguin Random House Australia Pty Ltd, 2018

3 5 7 9 10 8 6 4 2

Cover images: light - colbalt88/Shutterstock; landscape - benchart/Shutterstock; parliament building - stockish/Shutterstock; stars - Alex Grigorev/Shutterstock
Typeset in 13/15 pt Minion by Post Pre-press and
Penguin Random House Australia Pty Ltd
Colour separation by Splitting Image Colour Studio, Clayton, Victoria
Printed and bound in Australia by Griffin Press, an accredited ISO AS/NZS 14001 Environmental Management Systems printer.

NATIONAL LIBRARY OF AUSTRALIA
A catalogue record for this book is available from the National Library of Australia

ISBN: 978 0 14 379323 6

penguin.com.au

MIX
Paper | Supporting responsible forestry
FSC® C018684
FSC www.fsc.org

In memory of my mum

Contents

Warning

Not everything you'll read in these pages is true.
Some of the people here don't always tell the truth.
They promised they would, but they don't.
Just thought I should warn you.

Ludo Simpson

1

Mum

I'd never been on a plane before and I wasn't exactly sure of the rules.

Was I allowed to do it?

Mum would have known, but she wasn't here.

I decided to ask.

'Excuse me,' I said to a flight attendant. 'Can I swap seats?'

'Not now, sir,' she said, sounding a bit annoyed. 'We're about to take off.'

'Can I do it after?' I said.

'We'll see, sir,' she said.

I hoped the flight attendant wouldn't mind if I mentioned something.

'You don't have to call me sir,' I said. 'In year six we just use names. Mine's Ludo.'

The flight attendant glanced at the sticker on my T-shirt. It didn't have my name on it, just the letters UM, which meant Unaccompanied Minor.

Or maybe Unavailable Mother.

'Doesn't matter, sir,' said the flight attendant. 'We treat everyone equally here.'

Which wasn't really true. My seat was about three times bigger than most of the others on the plane. And I'd been offered a choice between orange juice and a freshly made smoothie. When I looked over my shoulder, I saw that most of the other people on the plane hadn't been offered anything.

I sighed. I'd been enjoying my smoothie till I saw that.

We took off.

I was OK, which was a relief. The first two times I went on the flying fox at camp, I threw up.

The seatbelt sign pinged off.

'Excuse me,' I said to a different flight attendant, a friendlier-looking one. 'I don't really need this business class seat. Can you offer it to someone who does?'

The flight attendant gave me an amused look.

'What an unusual request,' she said.

'It's just a good turn,' I said. 'It's what we do in scouts.'

The flight attendant leaned towards me and lowered her voice.

'I wish I could say yes,' she said. 'But it's against the rules. Sorry. Would you like another smoothie?'

'No thanks,' I said.

The flight attendant gave my shoulder a little squeeze and went towards the front.

I thought of Mum. What she used to say about rules. How they deserve respect, but how they also need thinking about. And how sometimes it's OK to break them, as long as somebody benefits and nobody gets hurt.

I stood up, making sure none of the flight attendants were watching, and went towards the back of the plane.

The further back I went, the louder the engine noise got. And the louder my nervousness got, thumping in my ears.

'Excuse me,' I said in my biggest voice.

A few people looked up.

'Has anyone got sore knees?' I said. 'Or swollen joints in your ankles. If you have, or a bad back, there's a more comfy seat up the front you can use.'

A couple of the people smiled. Most of them looked away.

'It's not a joke,' I said. I got my boarding pass out and showed them.

Nobody said anything.

Then somebody did. A voice behind me.

A very cross one.

'Resume your allocated seat, please sir,' said the unfriendly flight attendant. 'Right now.'

She was looking even more unfriendly.

'I'm just trying to help,' I said. 'Some of these people look very uncomfortable. Why don't you let them take turns in my seat, ten minutes each . . ?'

'Now,' snapped the flight attendant.

She grabbed my shoulders and spun me around and steered me towards the front of the plane. I wasn't sure if that was totally legal. Though these days, to keep us safe and protected, people in charge are allowed to be quite violent.

The flight attendant slid me into my seat and snapped my seatbelt shut.

'Any more trouble from you,' she said, 'and the captain will have to radio the authorities.'

Before I could explain the difference between causing trouble and doing a good turn, the other flight attendant, the friendly one, tapped the first one on the shoulder and whispered in her ear.

The first flight attendant snorted crossly.

'I should have guessed he'd be a spoilt brat,' she said, as she walked away. 'He's all yours, Regine.'

The friendly flight attendant crouched next to my seat.

'I just let Terri know who you are,' she said. 'Or rather, who your dad is. I was really pleased when he got elected last month. We definitely need more good independent people in Parliament.'

'Thank you,' I said. 'When Dad settles in, he'll probably explain to the Parliament travel agent that in our family we don't need business class seats.'

Regine smiled, then hesitated for a moment.

'I read about your mum,' she said. 'I'm sorry.'

I nodded, not saying anything at first.

Whenever somebody mentioned Mum, my mind was always suddenly full of her, and my voice always needed time to recover, even a year after.

'Sometimes,' I said to Regine quietly, 'people get sick and there's nothing anyone can do.'

Mum said that to us quite often.

She was very brave.

Regine nodded and gave my shoulder another squeeze.

'It must have been really good,' she said, 'having your mum as your cub scout leader.'

I nodded. It was.

Mum was a great scout leader, everyone said so. She was always kind and understanding and really expert at encouragement. She'd probably have given Regine a proficiency badge for being so good at remembering things from the news.

I was about to tell Regine this when Terri's voice came over the loudspeaker, making stern announcements about landing.

'Sorry,' said Regine. 'Got to go.'

She hurried away.

I stared out the window.

Below us was a city. It looked different to any city I'd ever lived in before, which wasn't that hard because I'd only lived in one.

This city didn't really look like a city at all. No tall buildings crowded together. No grubby smog haze. No narrow streets full of jammed vehicles and people in them having road rage.

On the horizon, the afternoon sun was making a row of hills glow in a very beautiful way. Golden streaks of light beamed across the landscape, which was a mixture of treetops and spread-out buildings and wide roads with hardly any cars on them.

Canberra looked like a clean and relaxed and happy place where a good person could do good things without getting trapped in a lift or stuck in traffic.

OK, two people.

I remembered what Mum said on her last day. She was so weak, I was worried about her struggling to get so many words out. But I could see how much she wanted to say it.

'We're a family that always tries to help,' she whispered. 'Don't let this stop you. Two out of three's still a family, right?'

Dad and me couldn't speak.

But we nodded and squeezed her hands so she'd know we'd never stop.

Ever.

I realised Regine was crouching next to me again with a scrap of paper.

'My son's in the scouts too,' she said. 'Here's the address of his scout group. Just in case you haven't organised one.'

'Thanks,' I said, taking the paper.

When Dad headed off to Canberra two weeks before me, he said finding a scout group there was top of his list. And Dad had always kept his word.

I didn't say that to Regine because I didn't want to spoil her good turn.

'Canberra's not a bad place to live,' said Regine. 'But you have to get off your bum and do things, otherwise it can be a bit boring. Don't tell your dad I said that.'

She gave me a grin and hurried away to prepare the plane for landing.

I stared out the window again.

Canberra, boring?

The capital city of the nation?

The place where the most important things in Australia happened. Where the really big decisions were made. Where the largest number of people in the whole country who were dedicated to helping other people hung out.

The largest number plus two now.

How could that ever be boring?

There was a clunk from under the plane. My tummy twitched for a moment. Then I realised the clunk was just the wheels of the plane doing what I was doing.

Getting ready to do our job.

'We've done it, Mum,' I whispered as the plane shuddered down towards the dark shadows across the runway. 'We're in Canberra.'

2

Dad

When Dad was on the local council back home, everyone in our suburb knew him. At the shops, so many people wanted to shake his hand, it took him an extra half-hour just to get Mum's prescriptions.

People liked him because he was cheerful and friendly and kind. Plus he helped them. Both as a councillor, and as a camping shop owner.

You should have seen people's faces when he showed them how to set up a folding washbasin.

As I got off the plane, I wondered if Dad had started helping people here in Canberra yet. He wasn't officially meant to start his job as a Member of Parliament for three weeks, but Dad didn't like to hang about.

Terri the flight attendant didn't like to hang about either.

'This way,' she said grumpily.

She steered me and my luggage trolley into a side corridor, away from where most of the other passengers were going.

'VIP exit,' she said. 'Get used to it.'

I was grateful to her for escorting me, but I wished Regine could have done it.

Unfortunately, Regine was rostered to flush out the business class espresso machine or something like that, and Terri wouldn't swap with her.

Terri led me into a room with lounges in it. Dad was on one, his phone to his ear. As soon as he saw me, he jumped up and gave me a hug.

'Welcome to Canberra,' he said.

'Thanks, Dad,' I said. 'I've missed you.'

I didn't really need to say that because Dad knew. But whenever we were apart, such as when Dad was on the campaign trail for his election and I couldn't go with him because it was a school day, we always said it.

We both reckoned we hadn't said it enough to Mum and we didn't want to make the same mistake again.

'I've missed you too, Ludo,' said Dad, hugging me even tighter.

Then he turned to Terri.

'Thanks for looking after my family,' he said.

Terri snorted.

'If it was my choice,' she said, 'he'd be spending the night in an overhead luggage compartment. Handcuffed. Sign here.'

Dad gave me a puzzled and concerned look, then signed Terri's form.

'Best of luck in Parliament,' Terri said to him. 'If you're looking for a good cause, Australia needs more youth detention centres.'

She walked off.

Dad frowned at me.

'What happened?' he said.

I told Dad about my business-class seat and how Terri didn't believe in sharing. Before Dad could say anything, somebody behind us spoke up.

'This is exactly what I mean,' said a man. 'This is exactly what I was trying to warn you about.'

The man, who was wearing a tight suit, gave Dad an exasperated look. Dad didn't seem surprised, so I figured they must know each other. The man was a bit younger than Dad, except for his frown wrinkles, which looked older.

'One tweet about that little escapade,' said the man, 'and we'll be hosing this bloke down all week.'

I wasn't sure what he meant, but I didn't like the sound of it.

Dad didn't like the sound of it either. He gave the man a look. The man didn't seem to notice.

'You're paying for my advice,' the man said to Dad. 'And my advice is that Federal Parliament is not a place for kids.'

Dad sighed, as if he'd heard this before.

'Where I go,' said Dad, putting his hand on my shoulder, 'Ludo goes. Subject closed.'

The man opened his mouth to say more.

Dad gave him another look.

He shut it again.

Whoever the man was, he didn't know Dad very well. When Dad said closed he meant closed. Except in the shop when somebody urgently needed a mosquito net a few minutes after five-thirty.

The man sighed and gave me a high-five.

It caught me by surprise and I had to move fast to catch it. This was my first day in the national capital and I wanted to be polite.

'Nothing personal, Ludovic,' the man said to me. 'Welcome to Canberra.'

On the way to the car, Dad introduced us.

'Ludo, this is Mike,' he said. 'Mike's my adviser.'

'Hello,' I said.

We shook hands.

'Glad your dad remembers my job description,' said Mike. 'Cause he hasn't taken a whole heap of advice so far.'

Mike was talking to me, but he was really talking to Dad. I had a teacher like that in year four.

'Don't worry if you can't think of the answer, class,' he used to say. 'We're all finding it hard to concentrate with the deafening sound of Ludo daydreaming and not paying attention.'

I wondered how Dad was feeling about being treated like a year four kid. Before I could check, I got distracted.

I saw the car.

When Dad told me we'd have a car in Canberra, I thought it'd be a Hyundai like the one back home.

Not a huge white limo.

With a driver. In a uniform.

It was so big, all three of us all fitted in the back seat without any squabbling.

'It's a Commonwealth car,' said Dad when he saw me staring at the leather seats. 'All Members of Parliament have them. Comfy, eh?'

He patted the seat.

'Don't be fooled by the lounge-room furniture, Ludovic,' said Mike. 'This baby goes like a rocket on the freeway.'

'As if,' muttered the driver.

I knew it probably didn't, but at least Mike was trying to be friendly.

We started to drive out of the airport, and got stuck in a crowd of people with luggage trolleys who were trying to get to their cars.

Mike gave a sigh.

'Hopeless,' he said. 'What's the point of having VIP transport if we still get bogged down in the electorate.'

I didn't have a very good feeling about Mike. If my job was to give professional advice, I'd try to cheer people up, not complain all the time.

Mike lowered his window and called out to a family who were blocking our way. They had lots of luggage trolleys and were eating takeaway food.

'Excuse me,' yelled Mike. 'Could you finish your dinner somewhere else please.'

One of the men in the family glared at our car, at our driver, at Mike, and then at Dad.

'Get a real job, you parasite,' he yelled. 'You fat-cat politicians are all the same, swanning around guzzling our taxes.'

I was shocked, and I could see Dad was too.

Even during the by-election, when people often got worked up, nobody had said things like that. Not even the people who wanted somebody else to get elected instead of Dad.

Other members of the trolley family were yelling at us now, and making rude signs.

Mike put his window up.

One of the women threw something, which splattered on the windscreen. It was a burger, with tomato, beetroot, egg and barbecue sauce.

'Great,' said the driver. 'Now I'll be up half the night writing an incident report.'

He started blowing the horn loudly and creeping the car forward.

'Take it easy,' said Dad. 'They're just trying to get home too.'

The family kept yelling as they backed away. Other members of the public joined in, their faces bulging and angry.

I tried not to feel scared, but I'd never seen anything like it. Not even at the footy.

We got through eventually.

As we drove away, none of us in the back seat said anything. I think Dad and Mike were as stunned and shocked as I was.

Those members of the public weren't just angry with us for interrupting their evening meal and their journey home.

It was worse than that.

They hated politicians.

Dad was great. He tried to cheer us all up with a tour of Canberra, but it didn't really work because it was five o'clock and most places were closed.

Luckily there were still a few things to see.

The roads were excellent. No potholes. None.

And the hospitals looked excellent too. We drove past at least two big modern ones.

I could see why Canberra was such a good place for the national Parliament. The politicians only had to take a look around to be reminded how much better they could make the rest of Australia.

The bike paths, for example. I'd never seen so many. Amazing ones with new tarmac and white lines. They were everywhere.

'Great bike paths,' I said, trying to sound like Dad had cheered me up.

'Spectacular,' said Mike, nodding. 'The number of votes they pull in, truly spectacular.'

I asked Mike how long he'd lived in Canberra and he said years, which was probably why he spent most of the tour making phone calls.

As it got dark, floodlights came on and lit up the big buildings.

'Quite a city, eh?' said Dad.

I nodded, but my heart wasn't completely in it. I couldn't stop thinking about the people at the airport.

Just as well the angry man who started the yelling didn't have a weapon. A big triple-insulated esky, for example. Imagine if he'd used it.

'Let's call it a night,' said Mike.

'One more stop,' said Dad.

A few minutes later the driver parked the car next to a big grassy hill which was totally lit up.

Me and Dad got out and stared up at a huge building that was gleaming white and silver in the floodlights.

I knew what it was.

Parliament House.

I also knew that most of it was inside the hill. The only parliament house in the world mostly covered by grass. Which said a lot, I reckoned, about our politicians in Australia. Just ordinary humble people who didn't need to be above everybody else, and who also probably enjoyed gardening.

Why would anyone hate people like that, I wondered, the chill night air making me shiver.

'This is where it all happens,' said Dad.

He put his arm round me and we gazed up at the big gleaming flagpole.

'I can't wait for you to start,' I said.

I imagined Dad standing in front of all the other Members of Parliament, taking an oath to do as many good things as he could for as many people as possible.

'Mum would be very proud,' I said.

'Thanks,' said Dad.

I could tell from his voice he was feeling as emotional as I was.

If it wasn't for Mum, we wouldn't even be here. On her last day, if she hadn't talked about us carrying on with her life's work, Dad probably wouldn't even have tried to get elected to Federal Parliament.

He'd told me that himself.

I looked up at him again.

'Two out of three,' I said quietly.

Dad tried to say something, but his voice was a bit overcome. He hugged me instead, and we got back into the car.

A couple of minutes later, as we drove past an area of trees and bushes partly lit by the streetlights, I saw something in the shadows.

A person lying down in a sleeping bag.

'There's somebody camped over there,' I said, pointing. 'I think it's a homeless person.'

Dad glanced over.

Mike didn't.

'I don't think so, Ludovic,' Mike said. 'Not in the national capital. We've got official shelters for that sort of thing.'

'Dad,' I said, 'let's just take a look.'

In scouts we always offered help to homeless people. Mum reckoned it was only fair. We don't have a choice about needing sleep, she always said, so everybody deserves a safe place to do it.

'Mike's right, Ludo,' said Dad. 'Anyway, we need to get your weary bones home.'

I was shocked. I'd definitely glimpsed a sleeping bag, and I was pretty sure Dad had too. There weren't many people in Australia who knew more about sleeping bags than Dad. Our shop sold about a hundred types.

I knew Dad meant well, putting me first, but why would he think I was too tired to help a homeless person?

All I'd done that day was thank Aunty Tess and Uncle Brian for having me again, let them drive me to the airport, and spend the afternoon in a business class seat.

I stared out the car window, wondering if Dad was in shock from the burger attack too.

That was the beginning of it, I think.

Things going wrong for us in Canberra.

3

Shock

There were more shocks that first day.

Starting with the house.

'Welcome to your Canberra home,' said Dad.

The car had just stopped outside a house that was at least twice as big as our house back home. This house was lit up, so I could see all the details, including a garage that looked like it could take at least three Commonwealth cars.

I was stunned.

It was an amazing house.

But I was also puzzled.

As we got out of the car, I tried to think of a nice way to ask Dad why the two of us needed such a huge place.

Before I could, the front door opened and a woman smiled at us from the doorway.

I was too shocked to smile back. For a moment I wondered if Dad had met someone in the last two weeks and fallen in love and got married. A kind-looking woman with grey hair and an elegant face. But no, I knew he wouldn't do that, not without telling me. And not for at least another year or two, for Mum's sake.

'Hello, Ludo,' said the woman. 'Nice to meet you. How was your trip?'

'He doesn't like business class,' said Mike.

'I don't blame him,' said the woman. 'Waste of money in my opinion.'

'This is Mrs Bayliss,' said Dad. 'She's going to be our housekeeper.'

That was a shock too. We'd never had a house-keeper in our family, not ever. Except for one of my ancestors in France who'd actually been one.

Mum told me that when the French revolution began, our ancestor gave up looking after other people's houses and started burning them down.

'Don't look so gobsmacked, Ludo,' said Dad. 'I think you'll like Mrs B.'

'Don't rush him,' said Mrs Bayliss. 'We need to get to know each other.'

She was right.

But I was liking her a bit already.

Which was a shame, because there was no way we could afford her.

We all went inside and there was another surprise.

Three other people were sitting in the living room.

For a horrible moment I thought they came with the house as well. A butler and a well-dressed gardener and a maid with a briefcase. But it turned out they were just political people here for a meeting with Dad.

'Sorry,' Dad said to me quietly. 'This wasn't meant to be till tomorrow. I'll get it over quickly and we'll have dinner.'

'Come on, Ludo,' said Mrs Bayliss. 'Let me give you the grand tour.'

She nodded to where Dad and Mike were sitting down with the visitors.

'On your right,' she said, 'people working too hard.'

She gave me a sympathetic smile.

I explained to her that Dad liked working hard, which was why we'd come to Canberra. To work hard at helping people.

Mrs Bayliss gave me another sympathetic smile.

I wasn't sure why, but I didn't say anything.

We carried on with the tour. It was a very luxurious house. The rooms were much bigger than I was used to and the furniture was all new. The TV was huge. A smart one by the look of it.

'What would you like for dinner?' said Mrs Bayliss.

I hadn't been asked that for ages. Mum sometimes asked me, but Dad couldn't cook many things, so there wasn't much room for discussion.

'Um . . .' I said.

'Ah, yes,' said Mrs Bayliss, looking amused. 'I see what you're saying.'

She pulled the UM sticker off my jumper.

'You might like to get changed first,' she said. 'How about I show you your room, and while you freshen up, I'll fix you and your dad some steaks?'

'Thanks,' I said.

I helped Mrs Bayliss carry my bags up the stairs, wondering how Dad could afford a house like this. I was pretty sure kind housekeepers with a sense of humour and strong arms didn't come cheap either. Camping shops didn't earn that sort of profit, not since Kmart started selling portable barbecues.

It got worse.

My room was like a hotel room in a movie.

I just stood there, staring at the luxury.

'This is your bathroom,' said Mrs Bayliss, opening another door. 'Careful of the towel rail, it's hot. And best not to turn on the spa till your dad shows you how to use it. Don't want you getting chewed up and spat out.'

She smiled and went downstairs.

I sat on the big bed.

Suddenly I felt sad. I was pretty sure Mum had never stayed in a house like this, and even though me and Dad shouldn't be here ourselves, I wished Mum could be here to share it with us.

I pushed the thought away. I knew how much Mum would hate to be spoiling things just because she was dead.

From downstairs came the sound of voices.

Cross ones.

For a second I wondered if the visitors were real-estate agents and annoyed because Dad was already behind with the rent. Then I remembered Dad had said they were political people.

More advisers probably.

I hoped they weren't annoyed about me being in Canberra. Like Mike seemed to be.

Tough if they were. This was where I wanted to be. Supporting Dad, even though it meant going to two scout groups and doing school online.

Dad would tell the grumpy political people to back off. He'd explain about him and me having important work to do.

A team.

Two out of three.

By the time Dad came up, I'd unpacked my bags, hung my clothes up, stared at all the empty space in the wardrobe, wondered if I'd be allowed to keep my bike in there, checked out the bathroom, had a pee, and straightened the perfumed toilet paper so Mrs Bayliss wouldn't know I'd been sniffing it wondering how much it cost.

'Sorry about that,' said Dad, sitting on the bed.

'Did you tell them to back off?' I said.

Dad gave me a startled glance, as if he thought I knew something I shouldn't. Then he covered it with a grin.

'Sure did,' he chuckled. 'Very sorry, I told them, hungry boy upstairs, so it's time to get lost.'

You probably think he wouldn't say that, but I knew he would.

Dad stopped grinning and looked at me.

'Ludo,' he said quietly. 'I know this must feel strange, a house like this and Mrs Bayliss living with us.'

I looked at him. Living with us?

'I'll be doing long hours in Parliament House,' said Dad, 'and I want you to be looked after properly. Specially with you doing school at home. I was lucky to get Mrs B. She's taken care of some very important people.'

'Thanks,' I said, and I meant it.

But what I really wanted to say was, 'Dad, why can't we just take care of each other?'

I didn't. I could see how much Dad wanted me to like all this, and I didn't want to spoil things.

Instead I just said, 'This house must be very expensive.'

'It wasn't cheap,' said Dad. 'But when I looked at how much renting a decent place would be, and how many months we'll be in Canberra each year, I decided that buying one made more sense.'

I stared at Dad.

He was buying this house?

A cold chill hit me in the guts. The only way he could come close to doing that was to sell the shop.

And our old house.

I tried to tell myself Dad wouldn't do that.

He'd promised that when we weren't in Canberra we'd be in our house back home, seeing our friends and helping the people in our district.

'One advantage of having a high-profile job,' said Dad, 'is that banks are happy to lend you lots of money. And us Members of Parliament also get our living expenses paid in Canberra. To make up for an MP needing two homes.'

I must have still been looking stunned.

Dad put his arm round me.

'I know this place is a bit flash,' he said. 'And I know Mum would think it's crazy. But after what you've been through, I wanted it for you.'

'And we've still got our old house?' I said in a small voice.

Dad looked at me. On his face was a mixture of hurt and surprise that I'd even ask.

'Of course,' he said. 'That house belongs to you and me and Mum.'

I hugged him tight, dizzy with relief.

I shouldn't have doubted him. Dad would never let me down.

That's what I thought at the time.

'Come on,' said Dad, standing up. 'Let's eat.'

He was smiling at me.

Suddenly, looking at him, I had a strange feeling. There was something not quite right about his smile. It was like somewhere deep down, Dad was feeling unhappy and stressed.

Was it the pressure of a very big housing loan?

That was all I could think of.

If only I'd known what was really going on. What was about to happen to Dad. Then I could have tried to help him.

4

Kick

The scout hall was locked, which was normal for scout halls on weekday mornings.

Dad and I peered at a note on the door.

It was about the next meeting. Which was on the following night at an indoor climbing centre.

Which wasn't quite so normal.

'I think I know where that climbing centre is,' said Dad. 'I'm pretty sure a bike path goes all the way there from our house.'

'Thanks, Dad,' I said.

He could be the most understanding Dad in the world. Knowing that a person wouldn't want to arrive at a new scout group in a Commonwealth car. Because scouts are meant to have initiative and self-reliance, not chauffeurs.

'Don't thank me,' said Dad, smiling and giving me back Regine's piece of paper. 'You found this place yourself.'

I was about to remind him that Regine had helped, but he put his hands on my shoulders, suddenly looking serious.

'I'm proud of you, Ludo,' he said. 'Including what you did on the plane yesterday. It was generous and brave. Specially with that flight attendant who should really be a prison warder.'

I smiled.

Dad stayed serious.

'Mum would be so happy if she could see you now,' he said. 'To know the sort of person you're growing up to be.'

He tried to say more, but his voice went wobbly and he looked up at the sky.

I had to let my voice recover too, so I did the same. It was the cleanest blue I'd ever seen. The sun was warm, but the air was cool and refreshing. In the distance, magpies were doing their funny friendly warble. I could smell gum trees, which was Mum's favourite smell except for sausages.

If Mum was here, I knew she'd like Canberra as much as I did. And that was even before she saw all the good things me and Dad were going to do.

Dad's phone rang. He looked at it.

'Sorry, Ludo,' he said. 'I have to take this. Do you mind waiting in the car?'

'No problem,' I said. 'See you soon.'

Dad gave my shoulder a squeeze and I headed over to the car that was waiting for us in the scout hall carpark.

On the way I passed another car, which wasn't a Commonwealth one, parked with its back door open. A woman was sitting inside, breastfeeding a baby. I hurried on, to give her some privacy.

A little girl playing near the car saw me and ran towards me.

'Is that yours?' she said breathlessly, pointing at the Commonwealth car.

'Not really,' I said. 'We just use it sometimes.'

'Can I use it sometimes?' said the little girl.

'Fraid not,' I said. 'Sorry. Your dad has to be in Parliament. Or your mum.'

The little girl looked cross and upset.

'That's not fair,' she yelled.

'I agree with you,' I said.

The little girl kicked me in the leg.

The pain made me gasp. As I groped for the door-handle of the Commonwealth car, the woman in the other car yelled at the little girl.

'Stacey, leave that boy alone. Stop pestering him. He's busy wasting taxpayers' money.'

I got into the car.

The driver, who was different to the airport one, gave me a look.

'Don't take it personally,' he said. 'These jalopies bring out the worst in people. Specially the clowns who pee on the wheels.'

I didn't feel like talking.

This wasn't fair. Dad had spent his whole life helping people. Well, at least since he met Mum.

Since then he'd helped so many, probably not even Bev, who does the book-keeping at the shop, could keep count.

So why shouldn't he have a car and a driver? It's widely known that you can help a lot more people if you don't have to waste half the day hunting for a parking spot.

I looked over to where Dad was standing, still on the phone, his shoulders hunched in a stressed way. Mike was probably giving him advice.

Suddenly I wanted to get him home before the little girl spotted him.

'If I had a dollar fifty,' said the driver, 'for every time I've sat in this car waiting for a politician to finish a phone call, I could afford to eat at the flash restaurant you're going to.'

I looked at the driver.

Restaurant? What restaurant?

The restaurant was on the edge of a huge lake.

'Surprise,' said Dad.

'Thanks,' I said, a bit stunned even though the driver had leaked the news to me.

We got out of the car. Ours wasn't the only one. About six other Commonwealth cars were parked there too.

It was the fanciest restaurant I'd ever been in. As soon as we went inside, a man wearing a bow tie took my puffer jacket and hung it up.

On a hanger.

And when we sat down and I looked at the menu, I was horrified. For the price of two meals you could have bought a whole set of saucepans, with lids probably.

'Dad,' I said. 'This is . . .'

'Relax,' said Dad. 'We're celebrating something important. We're celebrating that we're in Canberra, keeping our promise to Mum.'

I wanted to tell Dad we could have celebrated with sausages at one of the lakeside barbecues we'd passed on the way here.

Before I could say anything, Dad leaned forward and pointed behind his hand towards a man who'd just stood up at a nearby table.

'Government minister,' he whispered.

I glanced over. And looked quickly back at Dad.

The government minister was heading our way. He seemed to be smiling at us.

'Ah,' said the government minister, stopping at our table. 'The honourable member for Culliton.'

He held out his hand.

Dad half stood up and shook it.

'And this must be your junior adviser,' said the government minister, shaking my hand as well.

'My son, Ludo,' said Dad.

'And are you independent too?' the government minister said to me. 'Like your dad?'

I didn't know what to say. Scouts think for themselves, so I was fairly independent. But they also share their ideas with other scouts.

'Clever boy,' chuckled the government minister, giving me a wink. 'Keeping your options open. Hope your Dad's taking notes. Enjoy your lunch, both of you.'

He headed towards the door, stopping and chatting with people on the way.

Me and Dad looked at each other. I could see he was as dazed by suddenly meeting a government minister as I was.

I was also puzzled. What did the government minister mean about Dad taking notes? Dad didn't even have a notebook with him.

'I'm starving,' said Dad. 'Let's order.'

I looked back at the menu, trying to see what was the cheapest thing.

'Anything you like,' said Dad. 'There's two of us, but we're eating for three, right?'

I gave him a look.

Mum would not have approved of a restaurant like this.

'It's OK,' said Dad. 'I'm not actually shelling out for all this myself. It's part of my entitlements as a Member of Parliament.'

'Entitlements?' I said.

'They give me money,' said Dad. 'To help with my expenses. All MPs get entitlements.'

I thought about the plane ticket and the Commonwealth car and Mike the personal adviser and Mrs Bayliss and the perfumed toilet paper. They must all be entitlements too.

Suddenly I could hear shouting coming from outside the restaurant.

Through a window I saw a Commonwealth car driving away. The government minister, probably.

People were yelling at the car and waving signs. I couldn't read the signs or hear what the people were shouting, but they looked very angry.

Was it because the government minister had been spending taxpayers' money in an expensive restaurant with coat-hangers?

I thought about the angry and violent people at the airport. And the little girl at the scout hall, who had also been angry and violent. And her mother, who wasn't violent, but still quite hurtful.

The man at the airport had called Dad a selfish mongrel. And a fat cat.

The little girl's mother had accused me of wasting taxpayers' money.

As soon as we got home, I was going to find out more about entitlements.

5

Loot

I couldn't believe it.

If Dad thought I was gobsmacked when I first saw the house, he should have seen me in my bedroom later that day staring at what was on the screen of my new phone.

Ye gods, as Mum used to say.

It wasn't so much the two hundred thousand dollars a year an MP got as wages. That seemed a huge amount when I first googled it, but when I thought about it for a while, I was pretty sure Dad would earn it with sheer hard work and helping.

It was the entitlements that knocked me flatter than a well-folded tent.

There were just so many.

Business class airfares. All an MP wanted. Plus money for living expenses and postage stamps and computers and decorating their offices and staying in luxury hotels and printing mountains of stuff and paying other people to do part of their work and pens and chartered helicopters and negatively-geared investment properties, whatever they were, and cars and advisers and phones – probably including, I suddenly realised, my new one.

And more things, and more, and even more.

The article I was reading, which was written by a financial newspaper, calculated that an ordinary MP like Dad would get entitlements worth more than two million dollars.

A year.

I tried to remember how many MPs there were in Canberra. I was pretty sure Dad had told me it was about two hundred. I used the calculator on my phone to work out how much they all got, all of them together. Even before I finished the calculation, I knew it would be enough money to help a huge amount of people.

I stared at the number on the screen, feeling like the most stunned and amazed cartoon character you've ever seen.

Sheeesh.

No wonder so many people were angry with politicians. With all the loot and stuff they got that other people didn't.

Poor Dad.

It wasn't his fault. He hadn't voted for the entitlements. He hadn't even been in the job then. But people still thought he was a fat cat. And that was before they'd even seen our new house.

I flopped back on the bed, my thoughts leaping around like a badly tied tarpaulin in a high wind.

I didn't want Dad to be in a job where people hated him.

He'd be sad and miserable. Mostly because it's very hard to help people when they hate you.

Even when you've promised to.

A bit later there was a tap on the door and Dad came in. As soon as I saw his face, I knew something was seriously wrong.

He'd just spent over an hour in the living room, having a discussion with Mike. Their voices had got loud several times. Now Dad looked exhausted and unhappy.

'What is it?' I said.

Dad came and sat on my bed.

'I hoped this wouldn't happen,' he said.

I waited for him to tell me what. I could see he was feeling pretty bad and I didn't want to make him feel worse, so I tried not to look panicked.

'I have to go away,' said Dad. 'For a couple of days. Early tomorrow morning.'

At first I just felt sort of confused.

Dad was looking at me anxiously.

'On my own,' he said. 'I'm sorry.'

Suddenly I wasn't feeling so good. One of the first things Dad said to me after he got elected was 'where I go, you go'.

What had changed?

'I'm extremely new at this job,' said Dad. 'And there are parts of it I didn't know I'd have to do. Like fundraising trips to other parts of Australia. Tomorrow I've got to go up north and see some wealthy people who want to make a big donation. I have to go out on their boat for a couple of days and be pals with them.'

Dad didn't look like he was going to enjoy that very much.

'Mike says they won't be taking their families,' he said, 'so I can't take mine. I'm sorry, Ludo.'

'It OK,' I said. 'I understand.'

I was doing the breathing Mum taught me when she first got sick, and it was starting to make me feel better. Fundraising was good. Fundraising was money to help people.

'Mrs Bayliss will look after you,' said Dad. 'And Mike will as well.'

I stared at Dad.

'Mike's not living with us too, is he?' I said.

Dad shook his head.

'He's got his own place,' said Dad. 'But he'll be dropping in quite a lot.'

I must have frowned, because Dad put his hand on my arm.

'I know Mike can be a pain,' he said. 'But he's very good at his job. And I've asked him to help you with anything you need.'

'Thanks, Dad,' I said quietly. 'Will he and Mrs Bayliss let me go out on my bike?'

Dad thought about this for a moment.

'Yes,' he said. 'But only on bike paths and only with your helmet.'

I nodded.

Dad took a deep breath.

'Ludo,' he said. 'I meant what I told you this morning. I'm proud of what you did on the plane yesterday. And Mum would be too.'

'Thanks,' I said.

Dad didn't smile and I could see he had more to say.

'Mike told me something just now that I think is right,' said Dad. 'Things have changed for us. You're the son of a federal MP now. You're on show. You have to think before you do things.'

I nodded.

I could manage that.

Thinking was what I usually did.

I'd been doing it for the last half-hour, thinking about what I could do tomorrow.

To help Dad and the other MPs solve their fat-cat problem.

6

Tin

Next morning I said goodbye to Dad.

I didn't actually say the word. Instead we had one of those moments you have when you're feeling so emotional it's better to hug each other than try to say anything.

I didn't tell Dad about my fat-cat plan.

He was hurrying out to the Commonwealth car and it's hard to get new ideas across when the other person is rushed.

It'll be much better, I agreed with Mum in my thoughts, to have a quiet chat with Dad when he gets back in a couple of days. Then I can tell him how it's going.

I went to the garage and took my bike out of the cardboard packaging the airline luggage people had kindly put it in.

It was good to see it again.

I pumped up the tyres and checked the brakes.

I grabbed my jacket and helmet. I said goodbye to Mrs Bayliss and promised to stay on the bike paths.

Then I rode off in the crisp Canberra morning to help the politicians of Australia stop being fat cats.

There were lots of areas with trees and bushes close to Parliament House.

It took ages to find the place where the homeless person had been sleeping. I almost gave up. But I didn't because it was too important.

Then I got lucky. I recognised a section of road from two nights ago. After a bit more searching I found the squashed leaves and scuff marks under the bushes where the person had been stretched out in their sleeping bag.

But no sleeping bag and no person.

Which wasn't so lucky.

It was a big disappointment, actually.

'Excuse me,' I'd planned to say to the homeless person. 'Some of the people here in Canberra don't believe you exist, so is it OK if I take a few photos? When MPs see them, I'm pretty sure they'll decide to spend less money on themselves and more on people who need help like you.'

It was, I'd explain, what Dad called a win-win situation.

Good for homeless people and also good for MPs, because the public would be very pleased with how helpful and generous they were being.

That was my plan. Or had been.

Oh well, I thought. This is better than nothing.

I pulled out my phone and took a few photos of the squashed leaves and the scuff marks on the ground.

Which is how I came to notice something.

I saw that the flattened area which had been under the homeless person's body was quite small. Nowhere near as big as an adult would make.

I lay down next to it.

It wasn't even as long as me.

I stood up, a chill running through me, and not just because the ground was cold and damp.

The person who'd been sleeping here, alone and shivering in the Canberra winter night, wasn't even a grown-up, which would have been bad enough.

It was a kid.

Then I saw something else, next to the scuff marks, half-buried in some leaves that hadn't been flattened.

An empty cat-food tin.

For a second it was like Mum was there with me. Both of us feeling something we'd often felt in the past. A mixture of sadness and anger about how things just weren't fair.

'Don't worry, Mum,' I said quietly. 'I'm not going to stop.'

And I wouldn't, not till every MP knew the truth. That just down the road from where they worked, a kid had spent the night alone and cold.

With only cat food to eat.

It'd bring tears to their eyes. I knew it would.

And, I hoped, bulk warm-hearted generosity to their bank accounts.

Before I left, I cleared up the rubbish.

I crushed the cat-food tin and put it in my pocket along with some strange little metal pellets I found nearby. I didn't know what they were, but they would have hurt if somebody had trodden on them in bare feet.

I wondered if the kid had bare feet.

Usually clearing up rubbish made me feel better.

This time it didn't.

7

Harm

'Mrs Bayliss,' I called loudly as I hurried into the house from the garage. 'Am I allowed to make some Anzac biscuits?'

Mrs Bayliss stepped out of the kitchen.

'I'll need to make a lot,' I said. 'With quite a few extra ingredients. Nuts and seeds and chocolate. They're for people who need extra nourishment when it's cold. If you don't have all the ingredients, I can go to the shop.'

Mrs Bayliss put her finger over her lips.

For a second I thought she was telling me not to worry because she had every possible ingredient. Then I realised she was telling me to be quiet.

She pointed towards the living room.

I went over and peeked in.

Mike was in there, standing in front of the TV, the remote in his hand. His shoulders were so hunched, his suit jacket was puckered at the back.

His face was puckered too.

'Come in here,' he said to me. 'Sit down. There's something I want to show you.'

I went in and sat down.

Mike's voice was making me nervous. I didn't know what this was about, but I was pretty sure he wasn't going to show me a new comedy series he'd just discovered.

'What you're about to see,' said Mike, 'was on the early news this morning. And the mid-morning news. And it'll be in all the papers.'

He pressed the remote and Dad appeared on the screen, at the airport.

'First time I'm not there,' muttered Mike, 'and he forgets everything I've told him.'

On the screen a reporter with a microphone was asking Dad a question.

About me. About my business class seat. About how Dad felt about what I'd done.

'Proud,' said Dad. 'Very proud.'

Mike paused the news report.

'Did you persuade him to say that?' said Mike.

'No,' I said.

Mike gave me a long hard look.

'Ludovic,' he said. 'I know about lies. I work with professional liars. So don't ever try one on me.'

'I didn't need to persuade him,' I said. 'It's how he really feels.'

Mike snorted and clicked the remote and the news report continued.

Before the reporter could ask another question, Dad smiled at her, thanked her for asking the first one, and walked away.

The reporter turned and started talking to us viewers. She wondered whether this short interview told us anything about Dad. Whether, for example, Australia's newest Member of Parliament thought MPs should give up some of their entitlements.

'Yes,' I said to the TV. 'He does.'

Mike gave me a look.

OK, I was exaggerating a bit. I wasn't certain yet if Dad actually did feel that way. But I was sure he would once I pointed out how many hotel rooms for the needy the entitlements money would buy, and how many meals that didn't involve cat food.

I was about to explain this to Mike, but I got distracted.

Suddenly there was a photo of Mum on the TV screen. A Christmas one, showing her and me and Dad next to our Christmas tree.

I was shocked.

The reporter was talking about the tragedy in Dad's life, and whether it gave us any clues about how he'd deal with the pressures of his new job.

I wanted to tell her to shut up.

It was none of her business.

She didn't shut up.

'These are questions we don't have answers to yet,' she said. 'But in a Federal Parliament where everyone wants the new independent member on their side, clearly Garth Simpson is a man to be watched closely.'

Mike swore, which gave me a clue that he'd never been a scout. He turned the TV off, which I was grateful for.

'Where did they get that photo?' I said. 'They don't have any right. It's private.'

'Here's your first Canberra lesson,' said Mike. 'Nothing here is private.'

That was ridiculous. My bathroom door upstairs had a bolt on it, a big one, that I was pretty sure was gold-plated.

'I can see you don't agree,' said Mike. 'Perhaps your Anzac biscuit buddy can persuade you. What do you say, Mrs B? Would you agree that what I've just said is true?'

Mrs Bayliss looked at me sadly from the doorway and nodded.

'Your dad's not just a dad now,' she said. 'He's also news.'

'I know,' I said.

When Dad was elected to Federal Parliament, I knew I'd have to share him with the nation. But no way was I going to share Mum. Not when she didn't even know about it.

'Canberra lesson number two,' said Mike. 'Your father will have enemies. Every politician does. Your father's enemies will be looking for ways to hurt him. And they'll use everything that you do or say to damage him if they can.'

I glared at Mike again.

That was ridiculous too. Dad had never had enemies and he never would.

'Our job,' said Mike, 'is to protect your father. All of us, including you, Ludovic. Understand?'

He didn't need to tell me that. I'd have done anything to protect Dad. Like I'd have done anything to protect Mum if it would have worked.

'So,' said Mike, 'listen carefully. Stay away from everything to do with your father's career. Because if you don't, you could cause him very serious harm.'

I was speechless.

Not help Dad?

Clearly Mike had never been a member of a loving family, ever.

'Canberra lesson number three,' said Mike. 'Homeless people. I know they used to be a bit of a hobby for you and your mum. So of course now you want to help them even more. To keep her alive in your head. So you can pretend you haven't really lost her. I understand. It's natural. Everything people do is really for themselves. But don't get your father involved. There are no votes in it.'

I stood up.

I wanted to grab Mike and shake him till he apologised to Mum. And to me. Till he understood just how totally wrong he was.

Before I could, Mrs Bayliss spoke up.

'I think that's enough for today,' she said.

Mike looked at her for a moment, then looked back at me.

'Who are the Anzac biscuits for?' he asked.

'People I meet,' I snarled.

'Good,' said Mike. 'That's exactly what a kid your age should be doing. Making friends with other kids.'

He gave Mrs Bayliss a stern look.

'Make sure nobody is poisoned,' he said, and left.

Mrs Bayliss didn't say anything until we heard Mike's car drive away. Then she took my hand and led me into the kitchen.

'He could have said all that a bit more nicely,' she murmured. 'And left out the rude and insulting stuff. But some of it needed to be said.'

I didn't argue.

There was too much to do and I was running out of time.

I needed help.

This was a job for the scouts.

8

Henry

'Welcome, Ludo,' said the scout leader. 'Are you a climber?'

I looked up at the climbing wall, which was very high and covered in scouts. I looked at the ropes the scouts were hanging from and the harnesses they were wearing and the climbing shoes they were climbing in.

I'd never seen a climbing wall up close before. Or so much expensive gear up close, except in the pages of a wholesaler's catalogue.

'Not really,' I said.

'No matter,' said the scout leader. 'We do abseiling as well. And white water rafting and snowboarding and hang-gliding and three types of karate and potholing in underground caverns. Any of that appeal to you?'

'Not really,' I said. 'Mostly I do helping.'

The scout leader looked puzzled.

'Finding people who need help,' I said. 'And helping them.'

'Ah, yes,' said the scout leader. 'In this group we're very keen on first aid. Climbing injuries, rafting injuries, sprained ankles from hang-gliding. Is that the sort of helping you mean?'

I was about to explain to the scout leader about homeless kids eating cat food, when someone on the wall gave a terrified yell.

We turned.

A boy was hanging upside down, his harness hooked over a rock. He was kicking his legs and flapping his arms in panic. Luckily he was only about a metre-and-a-half off the ground.

Some of the other scouts helped him down.

'Just the person I was hoping would join us,' said the scout leader. 'Henry, this is Ludo.'

The boy, still a bit wobbly, peered at me. He wasn't wearing hi-tech climbing gear and an ultra-light backpack like most of the others. Just a normal scout jumper and scarf.

He gave a grin and came over.

'Hello,' he said. 'I'm Henry Tang. My mum told me you might turn up.'

'Hello,' I said, pleased to see him.

'Do you like climbing?' said Henry.

'Not much,' I said.

'Me neither,' said Henry. 'But they love it here and a good scout tries to confront his fears.'

He paused and frowned.

'But you don't have to confront yours on your first night,' he said. 'If you'd rather not.'

'Thanks,' I said.

I grinned at him. I should have guessed Regine's son would be friendly. And no wonder he wasn't very good with heights. He'd probably grown up worrying about his mum flying through cyclones.

Three other scouts came over, two girls and another boy.

'This is Wattle Patrol,' said Henry. 'I'm hoping to be their patrol leader one day.'

'And if he makes it,' said one of the girls, 'it won't be because of his climbing.'

'Wait a sec,' the other girl said, peering at me. 'I know you.'

'Do you?' I said.

I looked at her more closely. I was pretty sure I didn't know her.

'I saw you on TV,' she said.

The other boy's mouth dropped open.

'You're that kid,' he said. 'You gave away your first class seat.'

'Business class,' I said.

The three patrol members frowned.

'Why did you do that?' said the first girl.

'Perhaps,' said Henry, 'Ludo doesn't want to talk about it.'

The other three ignored him. They were giving me strange looks, like I was something they'd found wriggling on their plate at camp.

I tried to stay friendly.

'It's just the scout promise,' I said. 'You know, the part about helping other people.'

The three patrol members were still frowning.

'We don't do that part much,' said one of the girls. 'We mostly do the bit about facing challenges with courage.'

'Yeah,' said the boy. 'Climbing challenges mostly.'

'How would you feel,' I said hopefully, 'about trying a different kind of challenge? One that's just as exciting in its own way.'

Henry was looking very interested, but it was the other boy who answered.

'Definitely,' said the boy. 'Solo hot air ballooning. I've always wanted to give that a go.'

I'd never been on a climbing wall before.

Normally I'd have accepted Henry's kind offer of giving my fears a miss tonight. But I was pretty sure the other patrol members wouldn't come with me on a new type of challenge if they thought I was a jelly-blob.

Climbing wasn't quite as hard as I'd imagined, once I worked out that it was best to just move one hand or one foot at a time.

The mistake I made was leaving my backpack on. I did it because all the other scouts were climbing with theirs on, and I wanted them to respect me.

For the good of the mission.

Trouble was, me and Mrs Bayliss had really gone

to town with the nuts and seeds and chocolate in the Anzac biscuits, and I was learning Biscuit Lesson number one.

Extra nutrition means extra weight.

I tried to take my mind off the nagging pain in my back by thinking about something else.

I chose the wrong thing.

The thing Mike had said. About how I was only helping homeless people for selfish reasons.

Remembering that gave me a violent spasm of hurt feelings.

Here's a hint for anybody planning to go up a climbing wall for the first time. Try not to have a spasm of hurt feelings halfway up.

It can make you slip.

Like I did.

'Arghhh,' I yelled.

My harness saved me, but suddenly I was upside down and so was my backpack and it mustn't have been zipped up properly because I saw Mrs Bayliss's plastic container plummeting away.

It smacked onto the floor and the lid came off and Anzac biscuits went everywhere.

There was silence as everyone stared at them.

The only person who said anything was Mum, in my head.

'Stay focussed,' she said gently. 'Stay focussed on something that's more important than you feeling like an idiot.'

I pulled myself the right way up.

'I'm sorry,' I said in the loudest voice I could manage. 'But we don't really have time for climbing at the moment. There are people who need help urgently, and we need to go and help them.'

I clambered down and started picking up the broken biscuits.

Everyone kept on staring, except for Henry and the scout leader, who helped me.

'Give them more details,' Mum whispered to me as I put the last piece of biscuit into the container.

'Homeless people,' I said to the scouts. 'And MPs. They both need our help. If anyone wants to come with me, I'll explain on the way.'

I slung my backpack over my shoulder and walked out.

I knew that probably not all the scouts would be brave enough to risk facing a challenge with somebody who falls off walls, but I hoped a few would.

I waited in the carpark for about five minutes.

Nobody came out of the building.

I was too disappointed to get on my bike straight away, so to help myself feel better and get some energy back, I had an Anzac biscuit.

Well, pieces of one.

Then I got on my bike and started heading towards the bike path.

'Wait,' called a voice. 'Ludo.'

I stopped and looked round.

Henry was running towards me.

'Sorry,' he said. 'As a future patrol leader I prefer not to leave until the patrol inspection is over. And until I've helped clean the meeting venue. There were quite a few crumbs.'

I hadn't thought about that.

'I'm sorry too,' I said. 'I should have stayed and helped.'

'I hope you don't mind me saying,' said Henry, 'but this isn't really your sort of scout group, is it?'

I shook my head.

'It's not mine really,' said Henry. 'Not enough different types of challenges. My mum says instead of calling it facing challenges with courage, this group should really call it facing challenges with credit cards.'

I smiled.

'What sort of challenges do you like facing?' said Henry.

I told him in detail about my plan to melt the hearts of MPs and encourage them to share their entitlements around.

Henry's eyes went wide.

Not with doubt. Or scorn.

I was pretty sure it was excitement.

'That would involve map-reading, wouldn't it? he said. 'And getting to know people from other cultures and religions. We'd have to use our wits and our language skills and our compasses and our powers of empathy and all sorts of other traditional scouting skills.'

His eyes were even wider now. Definitely with excitement.

'Yes, we would,' I said.

We looked at each other.

Henry gave me the scout salute. I gave him one back.

'I'm happy to meet you, future Patrol Leader Tang,' I said. 'Would you like parts of some Anzac biscuits?'

9

Glare

Henry had lived in Canberra all his life and he knew exactly where the homeless people were.

Well, a couple of them.

After pedalling for about ten minutes, we turned off the bike path and rode down a street past some closed shops.

I had a pang of guilt.

Two actually.

Dad had said to stay on the bike paths. And I'd told Mrs Bayliss I'd be home by eight-thirty.

I decided this was an example of what Mum used to say about rules. There was absolutely no traffic on this street, so nobody was going to get hurt, and with a bit of luck a lot of people would benefit.

Plus my bedtime wasn't till nine-thirty.

Henry turned a corner into a small carpark.

I followed.

We got off our bikes.

'Torches,' said Henry. 'Remember, a scout always keeps his torch pointed downwards at thirty degrees so it doesn't dazzle.'

'I haven't actually brought a torch,' I said.

How embarrassing. I was so busy with the Anzac biscuits, I completely forgot about a torch.

'Two scouts, one torch,' said Henry. 'Link arms, stay in step.'

Henry really knew his stuff.

I'd never even learned this.

We linked arms and walked slowly in step towards the other end of the carpark, Henry keeping the torch steady at thirty degrees.

'Last month,' said Henry, 'me and my mum went to a restaurant round the corner for my birthday dinner. We parked here, so I had the chance to survey the territory.'

We walked in silence for a few steps.

'How did the other members of Wattle Patrol feel?' I said to Henry. 'Did they mind you leaving early and going off without them?'

'They weren't very happy,' said Henry. 'Sometimes I worry about upsetting them. I'll never get to be patrol leader if they vote against me. And possibly criticise me in the newsletter.'

'Sorry to hear that,' I said. 'Thanks for doing it anyway.'

'A scout tries to make the right choice,' said Henry. 'Even if it's the hard choice.'

In the torchlight up ahead, in the street at the

other end of the carpark, two figures appeared. One was sitting against a fence under a carport at the back of a shop, the other was lying down.

As we got closer, I saw that the person sitting up was an elderly man, glaring at us. The person lying down was also a man, but not so elderly and not glaring. He seemed to be asleep. Next to him was a large black dog, one eye open, watching us.

'What do we do now?' whispered Henry.

'It's OK,' I said. 'I've done this before.'

But not for quite a while. This morning there hadn't been a homeless person actually available, just a cat-food tin.

I took a deep breath.

'Excuse me,' I said to the elderly man. 'Would you like an Anzac biscuit?'

Something about the way he was glaring made me think this might be the best way to start. Leave the photos and the win-win situation till later.

I took the lid off the biscuit container and held it out to him.

'Doing a good turn?' growled the man.

I nodded.

I could see how thin the mens' foam mattresses were, and how their sleeping bags looked like they only had about a number-three warmth rating.

As soon as Dad got back, I'd tell him about that. Dad was brilliant at coming up with exactly the right sleeping bag for any climatic condition on any street.

The elderly man reached shakily into the plastic container and took a handful of biscuit parts. He put several into the pocket of the man lying down, gave one to the dog and ate one himself.

'Thanks,' he said.

'I'll have mine later,' muttered the other man.

I wondered if this would be a good moment for the win-win situation.

It wasn't.

'You've probably noticed,' said the elderly man, 'that we're not in the official shelter. Too crowded there. No privacy.'

'And no dogs,' said the man lying down.

'Privacy here,' said the elderly man. 'Until you blokes arrived.'

There was a silence.

I could feel Henry tugging at the back of my jumper. He was probably right. This probably wasn't the time for photos, even ones that would make MP's jaws drop.

But I couldn't leave without at least trying.

'Would you mind,' I said to the men, 'if I take a few photos? I'm trying to make MPs feel more sympathetic towards homeless people.'

'We're not homeless people,' growled the elderly man. 'We're street people. This is our home here, and it's called a street.'

'Sorry,' I said.

I still didn't want to give up, but Henry was dragging on my jumper very hard.

And there was one other thing I wanted to ask.

'Do you know any kids who are sleeping rough?' I said. 'And possibly eating cat food?'

'Eating cat food?' said the man who was lying down. 'You've been watching too many movies.'

'There is a kid,' said the elderly man. 'He doesn't like being cooped up, same as us. Prefers the feel of leaves under his swag. One of his spots is near Parliament House, but he spends most of his nights in Mount Costello Bush Reserve.'

'Thanks,' I said.

'Careful,' said the man lying down. 'He's got a kitten.'

10

Shut

Henry also knew where Mount Costello Bush Reserve was, or he did once he'd googled it.

A couple of suburbs away, clearly marked on the map and with a bike path all the way.

We pedalled as fast as we could.

Henry was probably as anxious as I was about being late. I wondered what time he'd told his parents he'd be home. It was starting to look like we'd both be late. Never mind, it would be worth getting into trouble if we could find the homeless kid and swap a large number of biscuit parts for a photo of him and his cat food.

And there it was, Mount Costello Bush Reserve, a dark hillside at the end of a street of houses. With a dirt road, glowing faintly in the moonlight, disappearing into the trees.

When we got to the start of the dirt road, Henry suddenly stopped and switched on his torch.

He shone the torch onto a piece of plywood wired to a post. On the plywood were some words scrawled in thick black texta.

SHUT
NO ENTRY

That was bad luck. But there was also some good luck. The Mount Costello Bush Reserve didn't have a fence.

Henry was turning his bike round.

'A scout respects notices,' he said. 'And signs.'

I explained Mum's rule to him. The one about rules. How it's OK to ignore them if nobody is harmed and somebody benefits. Except instead of rules, I said signs.

Henry thought about this, but he didn't swing his bike back round.

Then we heard a sound behind us.

We turned.

For a second I thought I was seeing things.

Next to the dirt road, a large shape was watching us from the shadows of the trees.

I knew it was watching because I could see its eyes gleaming.

Henry gave a terrified squeak.

'Come on,' he croaked. 'Let's go.'

Suddenly he was looking like he'd rather be very high up on the climbing wall, dangling upside down by his compass cord.

The shape in the shadows was very large.

Bigger than either of us.

We saw this when it moved silently out of the shadows into the moonlight, still looking at us.

We also saw what it was.

A kangaroo.

'Wait,' I breathed.

I'd never seen a kangaroo this close.

She was standing completely still, paws in front of her pouch, her gentle face slightly tilted, eyes still steadily on us.

'A scout respects all living things,' whispered Henry, his voice wobbly. 'A scout tries not to intrude on the territory of other species. I think we should get on our bikes and not intrude as fast as we can.'

Suddenly the kangaroo turned and hopped away along the dirt road. But only for a few hops. Then she stopped and looked back at us for quite a while. Then hopped some more. Then stopped, looking at us again.

I had the crazy thought that she wanted us to follow her. Was that possible?

She turned away for the last time and hopped out of sight.

Henry breathed a long wobbly breath.

'That was close,' he said.

'Henry,' I said. 'She wasn't going to hurt us. If she'd wanted to hurt us, our intestines would be hanging from that mailbox over there.'

Which probably wasn't, I realised from Henry's face, the best way of putting it.

'Come on,' I said, and got back on my bike and turned it towards the dirt road.

Henry gave a sort of whimper. I looked at him.

'There might be a kid up there,' I said, 'who needs our help.'

Henry still didn't move.

'A challenge,' I said. 'A real one, not an organised one. Are we going to face it with courage or what?'

It was hard work, pedalling up that steep dirt road. Soon I was sweating, even in the cold night air.

I took my scarf off and stuffed it in my pocket. By that time Henry had stopped whimpering.

He had a special strap for his torch that let him wear it on his head. As we rode up the hill, using our bike lamps to see the bends in the road, Henry turned his head from side to side so we could spot if anyone was camped out in the undergrowth.

Even when the kangaroo appeared again, Henry only slowed down slightly.

She watched us for a few moments.

I had another crazy thought.

That she was checking we were following her.

Then she was gone again.

'Coo-ee,' Henry started calling out in a loud voice. 'Anyone here?'

I'd seen this before at scouts. Some people go directly from scaredy-cat to extremely brave without even pausing in the middle to check their life insurance.

The next time our kangaroo friend appeared, Henry didn't even slow down. Not until we realised she wasn't hopping away this time.

She was standing at the edge of a clearing. Not moving, no matter how close we got.

We both slowed down.

And stopped.

She was so near to us, I could see her grey fur moving in the breeze. Her eyes were big and gentle. Her face was almost thoughtful. As if she knew exactly who we were and why we were there.

Suddenly I felt so emotional I had to take both feet off the pedals and put them on the ground.

The second I did that, she turned and hopped away and we didn't see her again.

But we saw something else.

'Look,' squeaked Henry.

I followed the beam from his head and my stomach went tight.

A man was lying half hidden in the undergrowth at the edge of the clearing. His head was turned in our direction and he was watching us, his eyes gleaming in Henry's torchlight.

I got off my bike and leaned it against a tree.

Henry did the same, and for a few seconds I lost sight of the man in the darkness as Henry's torch beam splayed around us on tree trunks and branches.

Then Henry was at my side and shining the torch on the man again.

I pulled the plastic container out of my backpack and took the lid off.

'Sorry if we woke you up,' I said as we went towards the man. 'Would you like an Anzac biscuit?'

The man didn't move or say anything.

He was lying on top of a sleeping bag, which was a bit strange because it was cold in the forest. But he had all his clothes on, including a coat, which in my experience of seeing homeless people in bed was quite normal.

I was pleased to see it was a thick warm coat.

People in Canberra, I thought gratefully, must donate really expensive things to charity shops.

'We won't bother you for long,' I said to the man. 'We were just wondering if you could spare a few moments to help with a project.'

This might be a better way of doing it, I thought. Don't mention the photos yet. Might even be worth putting them off until after we've asked him if he's seen a boy and a kitten sleeping up here.

The man still didn't move or say anything.

I knew that sometimes elderly homeless people didn't have hearing aids and couldn't hear you till you were very close.

But this man didn't look very elderly. About the same age as my grandparents in Scotland.

Then the man said something to us.

It was more like an anguished croak. The kind of sound a person might make if they really hated Anzac biscuits or helping with projects.

But I knew that was crazy.

Nobody hates Anzac biscuits.

Suddenly the man closed his eyes and his head flopped back.

He must be very tired, I thought.

Either that, or weak with hunger.

We took a few more steps towards him.

I wondered if I should rattle the biscuit container to let him know we had sustenance and nutrition for him.

Then Henry made a sort of rattling noise in his own throat and instead of shaking the biscuit container, I dropped it.

Because I realised why the man wasn't moving.

I saw what was seeping out from under his coat.

Blood.

11

Shot

Henry's scout leader was certainly right about their group doing a lot of first aid. Henry was brilliant at it.

He knew exactly how to check the man's heart-beat while I rang emergency.

'Alive,' he called out in a squeaky voice.

I tried to tell the triple 0 operator everything she wanted to know in the calm emergency voice Mum had made our whole scout group practise a lot.

Location. Condition. Instruction.

'Hurry up,' said Henry. 'He's bleeding badly.'

I waited till the emergency operator finished giving instructions about the ambulance.

'Thanks,' I said to her. 'But I can't talk any more. Got to help with the blood. I'm hanging up to save my phone battery.'

I crouched next to Henry, who was pushing down on the front of the man's coat.

'We need a pressure bandage,' said Henry.

Mum had trained me in first aid, so I knew what he meant. I also knew we didn't have one.

'Scarves?' I said to Henry.

While Henry took his scarf off, I dragged mine out of my pocket. Two scarves weren't a proper bandage, but they were all we had.

I opened the man's coat and tried to see where the blood was coming from.

I couldn't. Henry's torch was dazzling me.

'Henry,' I said. 'Two scouts, one torch.'

'Sorry,' he said.

He unstrapped the torch from his head and shone it onto the patch of blood gleaming on the front of the man's jumper.

His hands were trembling.

'Actually,' said Henry in a wobbly voice, 'I've just remembered something a bit tricky about pressure bandages. You have to expose the wound.'

We looked at each other.

We both knew why that was tricky. It meant moving the man's clothes without bumping him. If we jostled him, it could make the bleeding worse.

A lot worse.

'Try not to think about it too much,' said Henry. 'Sometimes a scout just has to do the necessary.'

Gently but firmly I tried to get the man's coat off. I couldn't even shift it.

Henry rummaged in the pocket of his scout shirt and handed me something.

A Swiss Army knife.

'Use the big blade,' he said as he shone the torch onto the man's front. 'The scissors are too small. But make sure you pull the jumper away from his body before you cut.'

I hesitated. I could imagine what would happen if I didn't pull it away far enough.

I took a deep breath, opened the man's coat wider, pulled the blood-soaked jumper carefully away from his body, and sliced through it.

The man had another jumper on underneath.

And a thick shirt under that.

By the time I got through to his skin, I was feeling less positive about the overstocked charity shops of Canberra.

The wound was exposed now, halfway between the man's tummy and his chest.

Blood was oozing out. Not pouring or spurting, but too much for a bandaid, even several of them, even the really big ones for gravel rash.

Henry gave me the torch and took the scarves. He bundled them into a wad and pressed them down onto the wound.

'Call anyone else you can think of,' he said. 'In case the ambulance gets lost trying to find us.'

I rang Dad. He didn't answer. I remembered he was on a boat in the ocean, probably miles from land without a mobile signal.

That left Mike and Mrs Bayliss.

I did the easy one first.

'Where are you exactly?' said Mrs Bayliss after I'd explained the situation.

I told her.

'I've already called triple 0,' I said.

'I've got another number,' said Mrs Bayliss. 'A special one. I'll call it now. Stay where you are, try to keep him alive. Help will be there soon.'

She hung up.

I rang Mike.

For a top adviser, he took a long time to grasp what I was saying. Then he took a long time to say anything, mostly because he was using so many swear words.

He told me to go home immediately. When I refused, he hung up.

'Anyone else?' I said to Henry. 'Your mum and dad? If your place isn't too far away, they might get here quicker than emergency services.'

Henry shook his head without looking up from his hands pressed onto the man's front.

'My mum's in Hawaii,' he said. 'She had a last-minute roster change. And my dad's looking after his sick brother in Taiwan.'

'Who's looking after you?' I said.

I knew this wasn't really the time for family chitchat, but I was concerned.

'I'm a scout,' said Henry, offended. 'I can look after myself. Plus I've got an auntie next door, but she doesn't drive.'

'Sorry,' I said.

'Help me with this,' said Henry. 'Put your hands next to mine and press hard.'

I clipped the torch back onto Henry's head and pressed both my hands down onto the wad of scarves as hard as I could.

'Not quite that hard,' said Henry. 'It's just the blood flow we're trying to block, not the oxygen.'

After a bit of experimenting, I got the pressure right. Henry checked the man's heart-beat again.

He was still alive.

I kept concentrating on the pressure.

And didn't stop even when we heard a siren in the distance.

12

Hot

I'd never been in a police interview room before. It was very bright. Just like in the movies. Except the police officer sitting with me was nicer than most police officers in movies. She kept smiling at me sympathetically.

It was good of her, but it didn't really help.

I was feeling too stressed. Wondering if Henry and I had done the right thing. Cutting protective clothing from a serious wound. Pressing a couple of not-very-clean scout scarves onto it. Possibly exposing an innocent man's internal organs to microbes and biscuit crumbs.

I tried to stop thinking about it. The man was in expert hands now.

The ambulance officers had said me and Henry did a good job, keeping the man alive. They hadn't mentioned anything about microbes or gangrene.

Yet.

'Come on,' I muttered impatiently to Mike and the detectives, wherever they were.

I just wanted to get the questioning over and find out how the wounded man was.

I looked at my watch.

Ten minutes I'd been in here.

What was Mike doing? The two detectives who brought me here had been ready to start, then Mike had said he needed to talk to them first.

Finally the door opened.

'Sorry about the wait,' said one of the detectives as they all came in. 'Let's get started.'

The sympathetic police officer gave me a last smile and went out. The two detectives sat across the table from me. Mike sat against the wall.

'More water?' said the detective, pointing to my half-empty glass.

'No thanks,' I said. 'How is he?'

'He's been shot,' said the other detective. 'He's still alive, thanks to you. They're operating now.'

I stared at the detective.

Shot?

When Henry had said that's what he thought it was, I told him he was crazy. Why would anyone shoot a homeless person?

'Talk us through how you found him,' said the first detective.

I told them everything I could remember.

When I mentioned the kangaroo, the detectives glanced at each other, and at Mike.

They didn't seem to like what they were hearing. I wasn't sure why, but it made me wish I could have kept her out of it.

'And when exactly,' said the first detective, 'did you hear the gunshot?'

'I didn't,' I said.

The detective looked at me.

'You must have heard a gunshot,' he said. 'You were in the vicinity.'

'Area,' explained Mike, which he didn't need to.

'I didn't hear a gunshot,' I said.

'Think very carefully,' said the other detective. 'A gunshot doesn't have to be a loud bang. It can be more like a crack, or a snap or any sharp noise.'

'I didn't hear any of those things,' I said.

I was just trying to be helpful, but the detectives didn't look like they'd noticed. They both did some noisy nose breathing.

The interview room was even brighter now, and very hot. I was starting to feel not very well.

I glanced over at Mike.

He was watching me with a grim face. Not doing any of the things he should have been doing. The reason the law says an adult has to be in the room when a kid is being interviewed by the police is so the adult can keep a loving or friendly eye on the kid and make sure the kid isn't being stressed or bullied into feeling not very well.

Mike wasn't doing any of those things.

I wondered if Henry was feeling this bad.

At least he had Mrs Bayliss as his interview-room adult. She wouldn't just be sitting there scowling. Henry was probably eating Anzac biscuits.

'Let's go over it again,' said the first detective. 'Everything you can remember from after you left the climbing centre.'

I told them everything again.

I explained how we probably wouldn't even have found the man without the help of the kangaroo, which meant she was as much a part of keeping the man alive as we were.

The detectives didn't look convinced.

'Think carefully,' said the first detective. 'We know how it is, son. You're just a young lad. You're sitting here and it's late and you're tired. Is there anything you might have forgotten?'

'Such as,' said Mike, 'when exactly you heard the gunshot.'

'Please sir,' said one of the detectives tersely. 'It's much better if we handle this.'

Mike gave an exasperated sigh.

'Such as,' the other detective said to me, 'when exactly you heard the gunshot. It's OK if you forgot before and you remember now. You're only human and we understand.'

'I told you,' I said. 'I didn't hear a gunshot.'

'You must have done,' said Mike, 'because . . .'

'Sir,' said the first detective to Mike.

Mike went quiet. Apart from more agitated breathing.

I didn't get it.

Why were they so obsessed with the sound of a gunshot?

It would be easy just to say, Alright yes, I did, I heard a gunshot. But that would be breaking the scout promise. Since the first day I joined the scouts, I'd always told the truth, even when I knew it would upset people. Even when Mum asked me if I was scared about her dying.

So no way was I going to start lying now.

'I didn't hear a gunshot,' I said again.

The detectives both looked at Mike. Luckily he stayed quiet.

What they should be obsessed about, I thought to myself, is finding the thug who shot an innocent person. It could be a violent maniac who hates homeless people and is planning another attack.

I didn't say that. My head was hurting too much.

'What did you do next?' said the first detective. 'After you found the victim.'

Slowly I told them everything me and Henry had done. I stressed that it was Henry who had mostly kept the man alive.

I also told them that near to where the man had been lying, there'd been a plastic food container that must have been his. The lid was off and I saw what was in it.

A tiny furry dead animal and a couple of small dead lizards.

The poor man.

Eating cat food was desperate enough. How hungry must he have been?

I stopped talking. I was feeling dizzy and weak. I just wanted Mike to take me home so I could lie down.

'At any point in time,' said one of the detectives, 'did either of you see any other individual on that hillside? Apart from the ambulance crew and the police officers.'

'Just the kangaroo,' I said.

The detectives gave me an unpleasant look, which made me feel even worse.

'And definitely no gunshot,' said the first detective.

I didn't answer.

They knew my position on that topic.

13

Carla

When the interview finished, the sympathetic police officer came back and led me out into the police-centre waiting room.

'Glass of water?' she said.

I could see Mrs Bayliss waiting for me, so I said no thanks.

'I thought what you did on that plane was really kind,' said the police officer. 'Good on you.'

I thanked her and said it was nothing.

'You were mentioned on TV,' she said, 'so it wasn't nothing.'

'Ludo,' said Mrs Bayliss. 'You poor love.'

She gave me a hug, which I don't think she was being paid for and I really appreciated it.

I was pleased to see her for another reason. It meant Henry must have finished his interview too. I hoped he'd had a better one than me.

'Where's Henry?' I said.

Mrs Bayliss frowned sadly.

'His interview's only just started,' she said. 'Mike insisted on being his support person as well.'

Poor Henry, I thought.

Then I thought of something else.

'Have you spoken to my dad?' I said.

Mrs Bayliss gave my arm a sympathetic pat.

'Mike tried,' she said. 'But your dad's phone is off. He must be on the boat already. Mike left him a message, so hopefully he'll get it soon.'

I hoped Mrs Bayliss was right. I really wanted to see Dad. And I knew he'd want to see me when he heard what had happened.

Mrs Bayliss was looking as if she was in pain.

'Love,' she said. 'I've been sitting here with Henry for so long, I've got to make an urgent visit. Will you be OK while I'm gone?'

I nodded. I was assuming she'd just be having a pee, rather than going to Melbourne to see her sister or something.

Mrs Bayliss hurried away.

I thought of Mum and how she always called a pee a pee and a poop a poop.

I smiled.

Good on you, Mum, I thought.

She could still help me feel better, even after everything that had happened this evening.

She kept on doing it for several minutes, right up until the waiting-room door opened and a girl came in with a police officer.

The girl had blonde hair that was sticking out everywhere as if she'd just got out of bed, and red eyes. Though her eyes looked more like she'd been crying than sleeping.

The police officer had her arm around the girl, who was about my age, so she wouldn't normally be treated like a little kid. Which meant something pretty bad must have happened.

I wondered what it was. I knew from experience it took a lot of crying to get eyes that red.

The girl stopped and I realised she was staring at me. Then she gave a loud moan.

'Ooh,' she said. 'I'm feeling dizzy. Quick, I think I'm going to throw up.'

She flopped down in the seat right next to me.

'I am,' she said. 'I'm going to hurl.'

I tried to make myself small. To make more room for her and her vomit.

The police officer crouched down anxiously.

'Put your head between your knees,' she said to the girl, pushing her head down. 'Get some blood to your brain.' She turned to me. 'Keep her head down there while I get a bucket.'

The police officer hurried away.

As soon as she'd gone, the girl sat up.

'Your knees,' I said anxiously, pointing to her knees. 'You're not meant to . . .'

'Shut up,' she said. 'You're one of the scouts who found the wounded man, right?'

I nodded.

'This is important,' said the girl, lowering her voice, but looking at me so hard it was like her eyes were yelling. 'Before you found him, did you hear anything? Did you hear a gunshot?'

I stared at her.

This was crazy. Her too?

What was going on?

'Think,' said the girl. 'Before you found my father, did you hear a gunshot?'

I needed a few seconds to grasp what she'd just said. Her father?

The wounded man was her father?

'Did you?' she said.

'No,' I replied. 'I didn't.'

The girl thought about this.

'OK,' she muttered. 'That's a start.'

I wanted to ask her what she meant by that, but I didn't.

Her father. This must be awful for her. I tried to think of something to say that might help her feel even a tiny bit better.

'I don't think too much blood escaped.' I said. 'We tried to keep as much in as we could.'

The girl lowered her head.

Not down to her knees.

Just low enough to stare at the floor.

'The doctors have put him in an induced coma,' she said.

I blinked. First aid like that was too advanced for me. If only Henry was here.

'They reckon if he stays awake,' said the girl, 'he could die. So they've made him unconscious to give him a better chance of living. But it's only a chance. It might not work.'

I didn't know what to say.

The police officer came back with a bucket.

'Knees,' said the police officer, pointing. 'Your head should be down there.'

'It's OK,' said the girl. 'I just needed a sec.'

She stood up, a bit wobbly, and let the police officer put an arm round her again.

'We'll try to make this quick,' said the officer, 'then get you back home to your mum.'

Together they slowly moved away down a corridor, the girl, the police officer and the bucket.

Mrs Bayliss hurried back in.

She peered at me, concerned.

'Ludo,' she said. 'You look terribly pale. Why don't you lie down on the seats. There's a hot drink machine out there. I'll get you a hot chocolate.'

She went out again.

I didn't lie down. Or put my head between my knees. It wasn't blood to the brain I needed. It was answers to the brain.

Why, for example, was everyone so worried about a gunshot?

What was going on?

14

Stab

I thought Mike might know some answers, specially about the gunshot, but when we got into the Commonwealth car to go home from the police centre, he ignored all my questions.

Except one.

'Can Henry have a sleepover?' I said, giving up on getting any other information.

'Fine with me,' said Mrs Bayliss.

Mike shook his head.

'Time for young Mr Tang's parents to start taking some responsibility,' he said. 'Lazy oafs couldn't even be bothered answering their phone.'

'My mum's in Hawaii,' said Henry, sounding hurt. 'The plane needs engineering work, so she's been held up. And my dad's busy in Taiwan.'

Mike sighed.

'Well,' he said, 'whoever it is they left in charge. Whoever I've been trying to call.'

'My auntie lives next door,' said Henry. 'But she turns her phone off while her nail polish is drying.'

'Henry can look after himself,' I said to Mike. 'He's a very experienced scout. He's trained in personal hygiene, eating for health and growth, the responsible use of cooking utensils, bed-making, lock and dead-bolt maintenance, household repairs and sensible sleeping habits.'

I was pretty sure it was true. If Henry had been in Mum's scout group it would be.

'And karate,' said Henry. 'In case anyone tries to break in.'

Mike snorted.

'As soon as we get back to the house,' he said, 'I'm ringing the child welfare hotline.'

I saw Mrs Bayliss's eyes go hard with anger.

'Mike,' she said gently. 'I imagine you've been using all your skill to keep Ludo and Henry out of the media after tonight's tragic events. Why don't we deal with this in-house? I'll take care of them both, it won't be a problem.'

Mike looked like he was going to argue, but he didn't. Mrs Bayliss's good sense was too good.

'Just this once,' he muttered.

'Thanks,' I said.

'Thanks, Mrs B,' said Henry.

I looked at him.

Mrs B? He'd only met her a couple of hours ago.

'It's OK, Ludo,' said Mrs Bayliss. 'That's what everyone calls me.'

'Except,' said Mike, 'neither of you will be calling her anything tonight. The minute we get home, lights out, both of you. And if Mrs B hears a squeak out of either of you delinquents, you'll be cleaning the steps of Parliament House tomorrow with a toothbrush.'

In the scouts we make a promise to be friendly, respectful, and to help other people.

Which was why I was pretty sure Mike had never worn a scarf and a toggle.

There were two spare bedrooms in the house, but Mrs B set up a camp bed in my room, which was very kind of her.

She gave Henry a toothbrush and I lent him a T-shirt with the badge of my old scout group on it.

'Are you both OK?' said Mrs B.

I knew what she meant. Getting to sleep after finding a person who'd been shot was something neither of us had done before.

'I'm fine, thanks,' said Henry.

'Me too,' I said.

'I'm here if you need me,' said Mrs B. 'Don't forget, I'm quite experienced. I looked after a minister for immigration once who had terrible nightmares about drowning at sea. Night, boys. And don't worry too much about the Parliament House steps.'

She closed the door.

Me and Henry flopped onto our beds, exhausted.

But not too exhausted to talk.

'Those detectives,' said Henry. 'Did they keep pestering you about hearing a gunshot?'

I nodded.

'What did you tell them?' said Henry.

'The truth,' I said. 'That I didn't hear one. What did you tell them?'

'Same,' said Henry. 'The truth.'

We agreed that the detectives hadn't been very happy hearing the truth. Neither had Mike. Which was all a puzzle.

'It's not like they need a gunshot,' said Henry. 'You know, to prove that a crime's been committed. They've got a homeless man with a hole in him.'

We looked at each other.

I felt a bit strange, and I think Henry did too.

It was still sinking in.

A real person. Someone's dad. So badly wounded that being awake could kill him.

'Who would want to hurt an innocent homeless person?' I said.

Henry didn't have an answer to that. Neither did I. Except one I didn't want to think about. The one involving a ruthless vicious homeless-person-hating maniac.

'Wait a sec,' said Henry. 'What if the homeless man wasn't shot? What if he was stabbed? That would explain why we didn't hear a gunshot. Maybe the doctors got it wrong.'

I thought about it.

'No,' I said, 'I don't think the doctors would get it that wrong. A stab wound would be very different to a bullet hole.'

'Not if you were stabbed with something round,' said Henry. 'Like a meat skewer. Or a sharpened chopstick. Or a thick knitting needle.'

I had to admit it was possible.

Then another thought hit me.

'What if there wasn't an attacker at all?' I said. 'What if the homeless man tried to kill himself?'

I'd heard about that sort of thing. Homeless people so miserable they just couldn't stand it. But saying that made me think about the man's poor daughter. Her dad wanting to commit suicide would probably be even worse for her than someone trying to murder him.

Henry frowned.

'It didn't look like a suicide attempt,' he said. 'We'd have found the weapon near him. Plus there's the other clue. Which the detectives weren't even interested in hearing about.'

'What clue?' I said.

'As we were leaving the clearing in the police car,' said Henry, 'I did some observing.'

I was impressed. I'd been so busy hoping the wounded man was OK, I'd completely forgotten that a scout is always observant.

'What did you see?' I said.

'Drag marks on the ground,' said Henry. 'Like something had been dragged across the clearing.

And I'm sure I saw blood on the drag marks.'

I thought about this.

'Maybe he stabbed himself on the other side of the clearing,' I said. 'Then dragged himself back to his sleeping bag.'

Even as I was saying it, it sounded very unlikely.

I was glad his daughter hadn't heard me say it.

'The drag marks were very straight,' said Henry. 'With two narrow straight furrows, like heels would make. I think if he'd dragged himself after being stabbed, the furrows would have zigzagged all over the place.'

I thought about this, even more impressed. Henry knew a lot about furrows.

'That makes sense,' I said.

'There were tyre tracks too,' said Henry.

'Tyre tracks?' I said.

'The person who shot or stabbed him probably had a getaway vehicle,' said Henry. 'Killers usually do. I memorised the tyre tracks.'

Incredible. I wondered if Henry's scout leader realised he had the world's best scout in his group. Possibly not if Henry really had as many nosebleeds on the climbing wall as he claimed.

'I'm sure the police will find more clues when it gets light tomorrow,' said Henry. 'They're trained to be observant too. Not as much as scouts, but quite observant.'

Henry was right.

We could leave it to them.

Which was a big relief, because I was exhausted.

We said goodnight, but I took a while to get to sleep. My mind wouldn't stop churning things over. Wondering if there really was a vicious maniac out there who hated homeless people.

I tried to take a leaf out of Mike's book and tell myself it wasn't my problem.

That there were no votes in it for Dad.

But I couldn't stop wondering what the maniac would do when he heard that one of Canberra's homeless people was a kid.

Sleeping on some leaves somewhere.

Completely alone except for a kitten.

15

News

I slept in late.

So did Henry.

I half woke up at one point and thought I could hear a TV voice coming from the living room. Talking about police and the Mount Costello Bush Reserve. I wanted it to be just a dream, so I went back to sleep to see how it ended.

I woke up properly when Mrs B brought us a cup of tea.

'Breakfast downstairs,' she said.

'This is like a hotel,' said Henry after she'd gone.

I told him about MP entitlements.

He wasn't surprised.

'My mum reckons MPs shouldn't fly business class,' he said. 'She thinks they'd be better off flying up the back. Keeping in touch with the people they should be helping.'

I agreed with his mum's point, but I wondered

if MPs would meet many homeless people up the back of planes.

We went downstairs.

'Fancy some eggs and sausages?' said Mrs B. 'You must be starving. It's almost lunchtime.'

I asked Mrs B about the TV news segment I thought I'd heard. Mount Costello Bush Reserve and the police.

'I recorded it,' she said. 'Not sure if I should let you see it, though. Probably not good to dwell on things like that. But I suppose you'll dwell on it anyway because you were there.'

We sat down and watched the news segment.

It was shocking. It left me feeling sick.

Not the blood or the violence.

The information.

'A badly wounded man was found last night in Mount Costello Bush Reserve,' said the reporter. 'The victim is in Lakeside Hospital in an induced coma, and has been identified as retired Member of Parliament, Vincent Moyle. Mr Moyle was a Federal Minister in three governments.'

I struggled to take this in. I could see Henry was stunned too.

A retired MP, homeless?

That didn't seem very likely.

The news segment continued. A photo appeared on the screen. It showed Mr Moyle with a younger woman who must be his wife, and their daughter, the girl I'd met last night.

'Tragic,' called Mrs B from the kitchen. 'Took them ten years to have a child. Carla's a really sweet kid. They've got a lovely home, and now this.'

Mrs B brought us our breakfast and told us Mr Moyle had been one of the best MPs ever. Generous and kind and tireless at helping people.

'Why did he retire?' I said.

'Politics has changed,' said Mrs B. 'The political parties want a different type of MP. No room for blokes like Vince Moyle. So they booted him out.'

I was shocked. An MP as good as Carla's dad, booted out just because he's old.

I asked Mrs B if she thought Carla's dad had gone camping on Mount Costello Bush Reserve to enjoy nature and cheer himself up.

She just smiled sadly.

'Thirty-two years in Parliament,' she said. 'One of our longest-serving MPs.'

That's when I started to feel sick.

I could hardly eat my eggs and sausages.

Mrs B was right about me dwelling on the whole thing. I couldn't stop thinking about it.

Not just about the things I'd seen last night.

About what I'd just realised.

'Make yourselves comfortable, boys,' said the social worker. 'Are you comfortable?'

Henry and I were lying on our backs on the living room carpet. It was quite soft, but I didn't feel comfortable at all.

I felt terrible.

It was good of the police to arrange for a social worker to come to the house. So we could, as she explained, let go of things.

But I was pretty sure it would take more than lying on the living room carpet to let go of the scary stuff I was feeling.

'Empty your minds,' said the social worker.

She didn't tell us how.

I don't think it would have worked anyway. My mind was so full, it was hurting.

'Think of a happy time,' said the social worker. 'The happiest time you can remember. And in the days to come, if you feel sad or scared, I want you to lie down and think about it again.'

I was lucky.

I'd had lots of happy times in my life.

But today wasn't one of them.

All I could think about now was the terrible thing Mrs B had told me after I asked her about Mr Moyle's pension.

'Two years ago,' she said, 'he retired with one of the biggest parliamentary pensions anyone's ever had. Not that it's done him much good, poor soul.'

She smiled sadly again.

Lying there on the living room carpet, I wasn't smiling sadly.

I was thinking about Mr Moyle's huge pension and all the other entitlements an MP would get during thirty-two years.

Millions and millions and millions.

Despite the kind social worker's encouragement, the sausages in my stomach weren't relaxing. They were tying themselves into painful knots.

I tried to untie them by emptying my mind, but it was no good.

They knotted themselves again as soon as my mind went back to the awful possibility I couldn't stop thinking about.

Nobody would have tried to kill Mr Moyle because they thought he was a homeless person. He was too well dressed and his face was too well known in Canberra.

But somebody might have tried to kill him for being a fat cat.

16

Fears

Henry didn't agree.

Which was easy for him. He didn't have an MP dad in the middle of a fat-cat hunting season.

'Calm down,' said Henry. 'So far, it's just a theory.'

I took a deep breath and tried to tell myself he was right.

We were sprawled on my bedroom floor. Not trying to empty our minds this time. Using them to find some answers.

Henry picked thoughtfully at the carpet.

'It is possible somebody tried to kill Carla's dad for being a fat cat,' he said. 'But it's also possible Mr Moyle has got other enemies who want to kill him for other reasons.'

I remembered what Mike said.

That every MP has enemies.

'Mrs B reckons he was the most loved Member of Parliament ever,' I said.

'You only need one enemy,' said Henry. 'Look how they carry on in Parliament. Squabbling and whingeing and being horrible to each other.'

I'd heard about that, but I assumed it was people getting worked up. Back home I used to lose my temper a bit sometimes at scouts. Specially when my patrol mistreated camping equipment. Particularly during Mum's last couple of months. But I never tried to kill anybody.

'We need to talk to Carla,' I said. 'Ask if her dad has ever had threats from anyone who hates fat cats. Any ugly incidents.'

'Burgers on his car windscreen,' said Henry.

I wished I hadn't told Henry about how angry that man had been. I was trying very hard not to imagine a vicious maniac sitting at home, deciding which fat cat to kill next. And remembering he'd seen one on TV. Who had so many business class seats that his son was giving them away.

I took a deep breath. Dad was safely in the middle of the ocean. Even when he got Mike's message, it would take him hours to get back. Plenty of time for me to warn him.

It was Carla, I realised with a pang, who was in more danger. What if the attacker was feeling grumpy he hadn't managed to kill a fat cat, and decided to kill the fat cat's daughter instead?

I told this to Henry.

He didn't argue this time.

'How can we warn her?' I said.

We grabbed our phones and looked in all the obvious contact places.

Henry knew much more about where to look than I did. Before I came to Canberra I hardly ever used social media for friendships. Mum reckoned you can't really get close to someone unless you can smell them and see their eyes.

It turned out Carla must have felt the same.

She wasn't on any social media at all.

'Maybe she just has her online security locked down tight,' said Henry. 'On account of who her dad is.'

That was possible too.

Either way, we needed to find her.

Lakeside Hospital had its security locked down tight too.

Henry and I got inside the entrance area, but we didn't get even close to where Mr Moyle was.

'He's in intensive care,' said the woman at the desk. 'No visitors. Police orders.'

'What about his daughter?' I said. 'Is she here?'

'Her name's Carla,' said Henry.

'That's private family business,' said the woman.

I wasn't really surprised. In fact I was glad that strangers, even ones in scout uniform, weren't just allowed to stroll into Mr Moyle's intensive care ward. Not with a homicidal maniac possibly on the loose.

'Plan B,' said Henry.

That was the one where we'd hang around as close as we could to the intensive care ward so we'd see Carla when she visited her dad.

In the lift, Henry improved the plan.

'We need to find a seat somewhere low profile,' he said. 'So we don't attract the attention of security guards or senior nurses with big syringes.'

We stepped out of the lift.

And froze with surprise.

Sitting cross-legged in the Relatives And Friends Respite Area were three scouts.

'Wattle Patrol?' said Henry, staring at them. 'What are you doing here?'

As well as surprised, he sounded quite pleased.

Wattle Patrol jumped to their feet and gave us the scout salute.

'We heard about what happened to you last night,' said one of the girls.

'My dad works in the ambulance office,' said the boy. 'So we knew it was you.'

'We've come to help,' said the other girl. 'To keep vigil at the victim's bedside. Except that we're not allowed to be at his actual bedside. But we've made the victim some Anzac biscuits for when he's feeling a bit better.'

She rattled a plastic container.

Henry was beaming.

'As your possible future patrol leader,' he said, 'I'm very proud of you.' He turned to me. 'Ludo, this is Bronwyn, Penny and Mattias.'

'Hello,' I said. 'It's good of you to be here.'

'We've never liked hospitals,' said Mattias. 'Not since I got concussion from white-water rafting and Penny stubbed her toe on a hang-glider and Bronwyn fell down a pothole. So we've decided to be good scouts and confront our fears.'

As Henry and I rode home, I could see how proud he was of Wattle Patrol. Henry was in front, so I couldn't see his face. But as he pedalled, his shoulders looked extremely proud.

I was feeling grateful that Wattle Patrol were on the job too.

It meant Carla wouldn't have to be on her own in the hospital, and as soon as she appeared we'd get a call. Plus Carla would get the note I'd left, warning her to be careful in case the attacker made another attempt.

I hoped she took the warning seriously. More seriously than the people at the police centre had when I'd rung to alert them.

I'd warned Wattle Patrol to be careful too. We'd agreed that if a maniac appeared, one of them would ring hospital security, one would ring the police and one would ring me and Henry.

Now we were pedalling home fast because of another possibility.

What if Carla didn't visit her dad? What if the thought of seeing him wounded and in a coma was more than she could bear? What if she trusted the hospital staff to do everything that was possible for him? What if she was at home with her mum, wherever that was, binge-watching quality TV drama to take her mind off things?

The maniac might know the Moyle family's address. He could be checking where it is on a map right now.

Wattle Patrol were doing a great job, but Carla needed extra backup, and that was Henry and me.

17

Slap

As soon as we got back to the house, I went looking for Mrs B.

She was in the sunroom.

'Mrs B,' I said. 'You know a lot of people in Canberra, right?'

She looked up from the plant she was watering.

'Quite a few,' she said. 'Why?'

'We need to contact Carla Moyle,' I said. 'Do you know anybody who has her phone number or her address?'

'Either address,' said Henry. 'Online or street.'

Mrs Bayliss sighed.

'Boys,' she said. 'I don't think that's a good idea. I think that poor family needs some privacy at the moment.'

I was tempted to remind Mrs B that this was Canberra, where there wasn't any privacy.

I didn't.

‘We’re trying to help Carla,’ I said.

I didn’t say the rest. That we were hoping to repel a maniac and keep Carla and Dad and every other MP in Australia safe, because that sounded too much to do, even for scouts.

‘Help her?’ said Mrs B. ‘How?’

I wasn’t sure how much to add.

‘Help her get through this,’ I said, which was true, but not the whole truth.

Henry must have thought that I was dangerously close to lying, because he spoke up.

‘And some other things,’ he said.

Mrs B looked at him.

I jumped in before she could ask him for some details about the other things.

‘We just think people should try to help other people as much as possible,’ I said.

Which still wasn’t the whole truth, but it was getting closer.

An hour later, we still didn’t have Carla’s address.

Then it got worse. Mike dropped in.

He sent Henry up to our bedroom, took me to the living room and started asking questions.

‘Was there anything you didn’t tell the police last night?’ he said.

I shook my head, shocked he would even think that. Mike had said he worked with professional liars. I didn’t have a clue what they were, but he’d obviously been spending too much time with them.

'I told the police the truth,' I said. 'Everything that happened.'

'What about when you were cycling through that suburb last night?' said Mike. 'Heading towards the Mount Costello Bush Reserve. Were there any sounds you could hear?'

'Yes,' I said. 'Of course.'

'Such as distant traffic,' said Mike. 'Car engines accelerating. Garbage-bin lids clattering. Back doors slamming. Music playing. Lawn sprinklers hissing. Phones ringing. TVs blaring. Dogs barking. Birds screeching. Babies crying. Children crying because they were missing their dead mothers.'

I stared at him, shocked.

'Well?' he said.

'Some of those things,' I said.

'Which ones exactly?' he said. 'Tell me which of those things you heard exactly.'

I thought.

'Distant traffic,' I said. 'And I think maybe a phone ringing. I can't remember exactly.'

Mike nodded.

'So the truth is,' he said, 'you can't remember what you heard in the thirty minutes before you found the victim?'

I realised what this was about.

'I didn't hear a gunshot,' I said.

'Answer my question,' said Mike.

'You're right,' I said. 'I can't remember everything. But I know I didn't hear a gunshot.'

'So in fact,' said Mike, 'there was something you didn't tell the police. You didn't tell them that your memory is faulty and unreliable.'

I opened my mouth to tell him he was wrong.

But he'd tied me in a knot.

Mike opened his briefcase and took out a sheet of paper.

'I'm sure you know,' he said, 'that if a person withholds evidence from the police, they're in serious trouble. Criminal trouble. Don't let that stupid flight attendant fool you. We've got plenty of youth detention centres.'

I didn't say anything. I was getting scared.

Mike sat down next to me.

He put the piece of paper into my hand.

'I promised your father I'd look after you,' he said. 'So I've written a letter to the police explaining that you were extremely tired last night and you made a mistake. All you have to do is sign it, and everything will be fine.'

I looked at the letter.

It was printed quite small and the words were hard to make out at first. Then I saw what I knew would be there.

. . . may have heard a gunshot . . .

'That's not true,' I said quietly to Mike. 'I didn't hear a gunshot.'

I was feeling even more scared. Mostly because of the way Mike was looking at me.

I did what Mum taught me to do with breathing.

So that I'd be able to speak.

I wanted to know why the sound of the gunshot was so important. But first there was something even more important I wanted.

'I'll sign this letter,' I said, 'if you give me Carla Moyle's phone number.'

I know. I'd be signing something that wasn't true. Breaking the first rule of a scout.

On my honour.

So the question was, would anybody benefit?

I was pretty certain they would.

Would anybody be harmed?

That was what I couldn't be sure about.

Mike was staring at me. He didn't look as happy with the deal as I'd hoped.

'You stupid little fool,' he said. 'You have no idea what you're doing. I've kept you out of this. I've protected you and your dopey father in ways you'll never understand. And you still want to stick your nose into everything. You little idiot. You can't begin to know.'

That was too much, him calling Dad dopey, plus what he'd said about children crying.

'I do know,' I said in a loud voice. 'I know what Carla's going through. I know what that feels like. Which you're obviously not capable of even imagining, or you'd try to help her too . . .'

I stopped because Mike was standing up and stepping towards me, raising his hand in a very threatening way.

Then Mrs B's voice filled the room, louder and colder and sterner than I'd ever heard it.

'Mike,' she said. 'I think you should go. Now.'

She came over and stood between me and him, looking at him. Not moving, not even blinking.

'Leave,' she said. 'Before I remember what you just tried to make an eleven-year-old boy do.'

Mike scowled, turned away, stuffed the sheet of paper into his briefcase and went out of the house without a word, slamming the door.

Mrs B breathed deeply for a few moments, then put her hand on my arm.

'Go and hang out with Henry,' she said. 'I've got some calls to make.'

In my room, Henry was twitching with excitement.

'I've worked out how to do it,' he said. 'How to find Carla's address.'

I sat on the bed feeling a bit shaky. I'd never been physically threatened by a grown-up before.

'How?' I said.

'It's quite simple,' said Henry. 'My mum's got cupboards full of duty-free whisky and vodka at our place. We'll get a few bottles, take them to the airport, find where the Commonwealth cars are parked, and do a swap with a driver. Alcohol for information. Those drivers must know where all the MPs live, even retired ones.'

I stared at him. That was brilliant.

But risky.

‘There are laws about kids and alcohol,’ I said.

‘What would your mum say about that?’ said Henry, his eyes shining. ‘Her rule about breaking rules? Which is the best thing I’ve ever heard. She’d say, how important is it that you speak to Carla? And we’d say, very.’

Henry was right.

It was very important. To warn Carla and find out what was going on. Even Mike thought there was something going on that Dad needed to be protected from.

‘OK,’ I said. ‘Let’s go.’

Before we could, there was a knock on the door.

Mrs Bayliss came in.

‘Thought you might like a cup of tea,’ she said.

She put a tray on the bed. Two mugs and some Anzac biscuits.

‘Thanks,’ I said.

‘You’re welcome, Ludo,’ she said. ‘And you’re right. Even in a busy important place like Canberra we should always try to help each other.’

She went out.

I looked down at the tray.

Next to the plate of biscuits was a small piece of paper. Written on it was a phone number.

18

Night

Carla answered the phone the fourth time I rang. She sounded angry. Probably because it was the fourth time I'd rung in two minutes.

'Leave us alone,' she yelled. 'No comment.'

'Carla,' I said. 'It's Ludo Simpson.'

There was a silence.

'Simpson like the TV series,' I said.

There was another silence.

'I'm one of the scouts who found your dad,' I said, in case worry had made her forget.

'And I'm the other one,' said Henry, pushing his mouth against my phone.

'I know who you dorkbrains are,' said Carla. 'What do you want?'

As briefly as I could, because Henry had his ear so close to my mouth I could hardly breathe, I told Carla about my deranged fat-cat-killer theory.

Carla was silent for a long time.

'Bull,' she said when I was starting to wonder if she'd put the phone down and had wandered off. 'That's total toilet water.'

I told her about the burger attack at the airport and the things the people had yelled at Dad.

'Yeah, yeah,' she said. 'Every MP gets that.'

I asked her if she had any idea about the size of her dad's pension.

'That's a bit rude,' said Henry, stepping away from the phone and giving me a look.

'It is,' said Carla. 'Mind your own business.'

'Sorry,' I said. 'I'm just trying to help you find out why your father was attacked.'

'I know why my father was attacked,' said Carla.

It was my turn to go quiet.

'What did she just say?' said Henry.

'Do you mean,' I said to Carla, 'that you actually know who did it?'

'I've got suspects,' she said.

'Who?' I said.

'What?' said Henry. 'What's she saying?'

Carla was silent for a few seconds.

'Come to my place and I'll show you,' she said.

'Now?' I said.

'Tonight,' she said. 'At midnight.'

For some reason, creeping out of the house late at night made me feel more guilty than if I was doing it during the day.

I think it was because it felt a bit unfair.

Mrs Bayliss was asleep and I wasn't sure if Mum would approve of people being deceived while they were asleep.

'She would,' whispered Henry. 'She'd love it.'

Henry was getting a bit carried away with the idea of my mum. I think he'd started imagining her with an eye patch and an ammo belt.

It would have been too noisy to open the garage door, so we carefully carried our bikes from the garage into the house, and then out the front door, which we closed as quietly as we could.

Outside, I shivered. And not just because the night air was chilly.

I was wondering who Carla's suspects were, and whether we'd actually be meeting them. I started to wish I had an eye patch and an ammo belt.

I pushed the thought away.

We put the address Carla had given us into our phone maps and set off.

It took us longer than we'd thought.

The bike paths were deserted, so at first we could pedal as fast as we wanted. But after that we had to find our way through dark streets.

'Sorry, Dad,' I muttered as we left the bike path.

'Look at us, Mrs Simpson,' said Henry. 'We're doing it again.'

When we finally arrived at Carla's street, we got off our bikes and wheeled them along the footpath, close to the hedges so we wouldn't be seen.

There were police, Carla had warned us, inside the house, guarding her and her mum. Which was good for them, not so good for us.

I checked the house numbers until we found Carla's place. We crouched out the front, staring.

It was huge. A mansion. A mega-mansion.

'I think I might not be a parking inspector when I grow up,' whispered Henry. 'I think I might be a Member of Parliament.'

I knew what he meant, but he was forgetting something.

If TV had ever done a lifestyle segment on this house, no surprise Mr Moyle ended up in the gunsights of a fat-cat killer.

'You took your time.'

Henry and I both jumped.

Carla stepped out from behind the garden hedge.

'Sorry if I startled you homicide investigators,' she said. 'I didn't want you ringing the doorbell. Apart from the SWAT officers sleeping in our lounge-room, my mum's sedated, and it's not working very well. Plus my grandmother, who's looking after her, wakes up if an ant farts.'

I nodded sympathetically. I knew what it was like when somebody in the family was close to death. Specially at night, trying to sleep. Trying not to listen to people crying. Trying not to cry.

'How's your dad?' I said to Carla.

'Still alive,' she said. 'Still unconscious.'

Henry, who'd been peering through the hedge at the house, turned to Carla.

'If it helps,' he said, 'there are scouts on duty at the hospital. They'll do everything they can.'

Carla looked at him, but didn't say anything.

Henry peered through the hedge again.

'Are they in there?' he said. 'The suspects who allegedly attacked your dad?'

'No,' said Carla. 'They're not.'

Even in the dull streetlight, I could see that her eyes were still red. Suddenly I didn't want to make things worse for her.

'We can leave it till another time if you'd prefer,' I said. 'If you've changed your mind.'

Carla gave me a scathing look.

'I'm not up this late for social purposes,' she said.

She went behind the hedge and appeared again wheeling a bike.

'Hope your legs aren't too weary,' she said. 'We've got a lot of pedalling to do.'

19

Track

Carla was right.

We pedalled a long way.

Not always on bike paths.

A few times Carla stopped under streetlights and peered closely at a battered old notebook with hand-drawn maps in it.

'Where are we going?' said Henry.

'Somewhere my dad knows about,' Carla said, squinting at the notebook. 'I think we're going the right way. My dad's good at maps, but his hand-writing's worse than mine.'

We rode on, Carla in front.

'Why does she have to show us the suspects in person?' Henry muttered after what felt like another hour of pedalling. 'Why can't she just tell us about the suspects using words.'

'Because,' called Carla over her shoulder, 'it's not that simple.'

'We'd understand,' said Henry. 'We're very good at understanding words.'

'I want you to actually experience the suspects for yourselves,' said Carla.

I wasn't sure if I liked the sound of that.

'We're scouts,' said Henry. 'We've got well-trained imaginations. If you just tell us, we'd get it.'

'No, you wouldn't,' said Carla.

We pedalled on.

The final time we stopped, it wasn't even under a streetlight. There weren't any streetlights.

We were at the very edge of Canberra, where the streets ended.

Carla was peering along a dirt side-road.

'Are we there yet?' said Henry.

'Shhhh,' said Carla.

She was listening for something. At first I wasn't sure what. Then I heard it. The distant sound of voices chanting and yelling.

'Sorry about the long trip,' muttered Carla. 'At least it's the right night.'

I peered along the dirt road, but there wasn't enough moonlight to see very far.

'Come on,' said Carla. 'Quietly.'

'We're trained to be quiet,' whispered Henry.

'Good,' said Carla. 'Because if we're not quiet, we'll be arrested.'

She got off her bike and started wheeling it along the dirt road.

Henry was hesitating.

I gave him the scout salute, he gave me one back, and we followed.

After a short way, Carla turned off the dirt road and wheeled her bike up a narrow bush track.

We did too.

The track led up onto a ridge that ran alongside the road below. The track was dark and bumpy, and we kept getting slapped in the face by branches.

'Easy to see she's not a scout,' muttered Henry. 'Zero branch awareness.'

I could tell we were getting closer to the people who were yelling and chanting because their voices were getting louder.

By the time we got close enough to see them, they'd started singing.

We crouched out of sight, peering down at a group of about twenty people. They were gathered in front of a gate that was part of a high mesh fence running along the other side of the road.

Most of the people were holding placards over their heads, like demonstrators. The placards were facing away from us and the singing was more like humming, so I wasn't exactly sure what they were demonstrating about.

But I could see why they were in such a tight group. Several police officers were standing around them with torches, stopping them going anywhere.

Carla signalled for me and Henry to keep following her along the bush track.

We crept along it with our bikes for what felt like ages. The humming got fainter and fainter until we could hardly hear it. I was starting to feel fainter and fainter too, with weariness.

Suddenly Carla raised her hand and we stopped.

She pointed.

Parked below us, on the other side of the mesh fence, was a truck. A battered tip truck, rear flap down, standing empty. There didn't seem to be any people in it or around it.

Carla pushed her bike under some bushes.

Henry and I did the same.

We followed Carla across the track and crawled after her under another clump of bushes. She lay on her tummy and peered at something beyond the fence. Henry and I peered as well.

I didn't have a clue what we were looking for. The moon was bright now and I could see that on the other side of the fence was mostly grassy scrub with bushes but not many trees.

Then I saw something else.

Shadowy figures in the distance. Some tall and elegant, some bending low. Some moving a few steps. Some hopping.

'Kangaroos,' I breathed.

'Shhhh,' said Carla.

There were at least ten of them. No, probably twenty. Silent on the misty ground.

Looking around. Eating the grass.

It was amazing how quiet they were.

All I could hear was silence and the faint shrill of insects and the even fainter shrill of people singing a long way away.

Suddenly I felt like I'd been slapped in the face.

Not by a branch. By an explosion of light.

A floodlight.

The kangaroos stood frozen, ears alert, staring in the direction the light was coming from, their bodies raised, their faces puzzled.

'What's going on?' whispered Henry.

Carla signalled to us to be quiet.

Then something strange happened.

Several of the kangaroos fell over. I saw them do it. And heard them. A thump as each one fell. The only sound.

More fell.

Thump. Thump. Thump. Thump.

'What's happening?' I said, not liking this.

'Shhhh,' Carla said. She didn't look as if she was liking it either.

The fallen kangaroos weren't moving.

More were falling.

Thump. Thump. Thump. Thump.

Others were trying to hop away.

They fell too.

'It's called a cull,' said Carla quietly. 'Professional shooters with high-powered hunting rifles. Night scopes. And silencers.'

'I can't watch,' said Henry, wriggling backwards.

'Stay out of sight,' hissed Carla.

My brain was going thump, thump too.

Silencers. I knew what silencers were from crime movies. Pieces of equipment that allowed a gun to kill silently.

'What's a cull?' I said to Carla.

'It sounds a bit like kill,' she said, 'because that's what it is. The authorities want to keep kangaroo numbers under control. Canberra residents want that too, but they don't want to know about it. So sometimes silencers are used. Even though they're technically illegal.'

I stared at Carla, taking this in.

'My father's writing a book about it,' she said quietly. 'To make all the information available. He's been working on the book for more than a year. A few weeks ago, at a conference, he mentioned the book in public for the first time.'

I started to understand.

No wonder the authorities were desperate for us to have heard a gunshot. Without one, people might think Mr Moyle was shot by a gun with a silencer. The trigger pulled, they might think, by somebody from this secret and ruthless kangaroo cull. In an attempt to silence Carla's dad.

Carla was watching me closely.

'I know what you're thinking,' she said. 'It's not that simple.'

Before she could say anything else, we heard the sound of a vehicle in the distance.

I peered towards it.

The vehicle, smaller than the truck parked nearby, was moving across the grass towards the kangaroos. A ute, by the look of it. With spotlights aimed at the fallen animals.

'Where's Henry?' said Carla.

I'd forgotten about Henry. I peered around, hoping to see him cowering next to the bikes or hiding his face against a tree.

I couldn't see him anywhere.

'Henry,' I called in a loud whisper.

'I hope he's not as dopey as he seems,' muttered Carla. 'The cops come down hard on people who interfere with the cull.'

'Henry's a scout,' I said, partly to her and partly to myself. 'He's trained to be sensible.'

Another flash of light caught my eye.

Much smaller than the spotlights. Near to where the truck was parked. Lots of flashes, close to the ground. Next to a hole that seemed to have been cut in the fence.

The more I squinted at the new light, the more my tummy twisted with fear. Because now I could see exactly what was making the flashes.

A small figure on his hands and knees with a torch strapped to his head.

20

Truck

'Henry,' I hissed as I reached him and turned his torch off. 'Are you crazy?'

'I'm being observant,' protested Henry.

'You're being an idiot,' panted Carla, arriving at a crouching run. 'If they see that hole in the fence, you're history. How did you do it, anyway?'

I knew exactly what Henry would say as he was being led away to a juvenile detention centre.

'A scout always carries the correct tools.'

He wasn't saying that now.

'Look at these tyre tracks,' he said excitedly to Carla, pointing in the moonlight. 'They're like the ones at the place we found your dad. The same tyres. Well, the same brand. OK, a similar brand.'

I had a sudden urge to switch the torch back on and take a closer look. If we were going to prove that a kangaroo shooter had shot Carla's dad, we needed all the evidence we could find.

But I didn't get the chance.

'Poop,' said Carla.

She grabbed me and pointed.

In the distance, across the scrub, but not far away, headlight beams were coming towards us.

'It's the ute,' said Carla.

No time to run. No time for us to get back to our hiding place in the bushes.

'Under the truck,' I said.

We all crawled under the truck and lay as flat and still as we could.

I peered out, watching the ute come closer.

'They don't seem to be speeding up,' I said. 'I don't think they've seen us.'

'Yet,' said Carla.

We all tried to squeeze ourselves even flatter on the ground.

The ute stopped right next to the truck. We were too low down to see everything, but as people got out and doors slammed, I saw three pairs of boots walking around.

Men's voices started saying things like 'big one first' and 'grab the tail' and 'on the count of three'.

Then I heard heaving and grunting, and a loud thump in the truck above us.

A couple of moments later, another big thump.

I wriggled towards the edge of the truck to get a better look. I was distracted by Carla grabbing my foot, trying to drag me back, but I glimpsed enough to realise what was going on.

The three men were heaving the dead bodies of kangaroos from the ute into the truck.

Thump. Thump. Thump.

Much louder than the thumps out in the scrub. And each time, the suspension of the old truck gave a sad squeak.

'What are we going to do?' whispered Henry.

His voice was a sad squeak too.

'Be ready,' said Carla. 'When the ute goes to get the next lot, we'll run for it.'

One of the men called to the others.

'Just a final load, I reckon.'

'I'm sitting this one out,' said another voice. 'My back's stuffed. I'm only meant to be the driver, remember?'

'Bludger,' said a third voice.

The doors of the ute slammed and it drove off.

Henry tensed up, getting ready to run.

'Wait,' I whispered. 'One of them's still here.'

An aluminium camping chair, an Ezycline Frontiersman by the looks of it, was being unfolded near the truck's front wheels. One of the men plonked down into it.

We could see his jeans and the bottom half of his checked shirt. All he'd have to do was lean forward to scratch his ankle or flick a piece of kangaroo fur off his boot and he'd see us.

We squirmed as far away as we could from him.

The man made a phone call. He started talking about football and how people who supported the

Canberra Raiders were more intelligent than the supporters of any other club.

'OK,' whispered Carla. 'Who's the fastest runner out of us three?'

I shrugged. I was average.

Henry, I suspected, was below average.

'I'm below average,' said Henry.

'I can run a kilometre in twelve minutes,' said Carla. 'From the size of that bloke's tummy, he probably couldn't do it in twenty. So I'll distract him and make him chase me. You two get away, bring the bikes to the last suburb we came through, we'll text and meet up.'

My head was spinning, taking all this in.

Thinking about how dangerous it sounded.

Carla didn't wait to discuss it.

'Give me a couple of minutes to get him well away,' she said, 'then run for it.'

Carla pulled her boots off, probably so she could run faster, and started wriggling towards the other side of the truck, in the direction of the man. Just before she got to the edge of the truck, I saw something drop down between the man's feet.

The wooden end of a rifle.

He must have picked up a gun.

I lunged forward, trying to grab Carla's ankle.

'Wait,' I hissed.

Too late.

Carla rolled out from under the truck, jumped to her feet and started yelling at the man.

'Save the kangaroos. Save the kangaroos. The Raiders are pathetic.'

The man swore in a surprised voice.

Then his feet flew up into the air. He'd been rocking back on his Ezycline Frontiersman and it must have flipped over backwards.

Which meant he was on the ground.

Which gave me a chance to get out from under the truck and onto my feet so I could fling myself at him and spoil his aim.

Frantically I clawed my way towards him.

As I got closer to the edge of the truck, I saw the man trying to scramble to his feet. Carla was still yelling at him. She hadn't started running.

Couldn't she see he had a gun?

The man's feet were tangled up in the legs of the Ezycline. He tried to kick it away.

There was a loud crack.

With a painful jolt of fear I remembered what a detective had told me.

A gunshot could sound like a loud crack.

Henry gave an anguished squeak.

The man swore again. His feet were still tangled up in the Ezycline, and I went weak with relief when I saw what had happened.

The crack wasn't a gunshot.

The rifle was on the ground, under the front legs of the Ezycline. The man must have trodden on it. The sighting scope on top of the rifle was shattered. Bits of broken glass lay on the ground.

I saw Carla's legs running past the man.

She almost tripped, staggered, then ran on, one boot in each hand.

The man took a few more moments to get his feet untangled, then went after her. I heard him thudding away, still swearing.

I stuck my head out.

Carla was already on the other side of the fence, running up the slope towards the bush track. The man was going after her, but not as fast and a long way behind.

'Come on,' I said to Henry.

'Give her another minute,' said Henry. 'To get him further away. Then we'll run for it.'

'We don't need another minute,' I said. 'Because we're not going to run for it.'

'What are we going to do?' said Henry, looking alarmed.

'Collect evidence,' I said.

Henry pulled out his phone.

'Not just photo evidence,' I said. 'Real evidence.'

21

Trick

We had to move fast.

The truck driver probably wouldn't chase Carla for very long. Only until he lost interest or got a stitch, and that could happen very soon.

Plus the other hunters in the ute could be back at any time.

If me and Henry hadn't been so rushed, if we hadn't been too panicked to even think straight, I'd probably have dropped the idea.

Yes, this was very excellent evidence. A heap of poor dead kangaroos that had been shot with probably the same type of bullet from the same type of gun as Carla's dad.

But stealing a dead kangaroo turned out to be so much more difficult than I'd thought.

Henry and I climbed up onto the mudguard of the truck and tried with all our strength to drag a kangaroo body out of the back and over the side.

Too heavy.

I climbed into the back of the truck. I hated doing it, for the kangaroos' sake as well as mine, but it was the only way.

'Sorry,' I said to them as I trod on them as gently as I could.

I lifted and Henry dragged.

Still no good.

'There must be a trick to this,' I said. 'Some sort of technique they forgot to teach us at scouts.'

Henry joined me in the back of the truck and we both tried to half roll and half lift the kangaroo. We'd chosen the smallest one we could find, but we still couldn't get it over the edge of the truck.

I realised Henry was saying something quietly to himself, over and over.

'A scout never gives up. A scout never gives up. A scout never gives up.'

Then suddenly our pushing and rolling and lifting worked, and the kangaroo flopped over the side of the truck and down onto the ground.

Henry and I jumped after it. I grabbed both its feet and Henry grabbed its tail.

'Sorry,' I said to it.

We started dragging.

'The best place to hide something,' panted Henry, 'is where people least expect.'

'Where's that?' I said.

'I don't know,' he said. 'I don't know much about kangaroos.'

'How about Carla's place?' I said.

Henry thought about this, frowning.

Then he nodded.

'Brilliant,' he said.

The hardest part was getting the kangaroo through the fence hole and up the slope to the bush track.

I'd have given anything for a high-quality tarpaulin-backed groundsheet to drag it on.

Instead we had to get it up the slope using a different method. Lifting it and almost wrenching our arms out of their sockets.

'This is great evidence,' Henry said.

It was good of him to try to cheer us both up.

I was trying not to look at the bullet hole between the poor kangaroo's eyes. It was difficult, because I wanted to look at the kangaroo's face.

Gentle and sad-looking in the moonlight.

I was remembering the kangaroo who'd helped us find Carla's dad. Had she been culled? I didn't want to think about it.

Finally, panting, we reached the bush track.

'I need a rest,' I said. 'I wish we had a trolley for the rest of the trip.'

'A scout makes do,' said Henry. 'We've got bikes.'

Henry's idea was very clever.

His bike and my bike side by side, with Carla's bike lying across both our handlebars, and the kangaroo on top of it.

'I call it the three-bike transport system,' said Henry. 'It could be very helpful to scouts and other people all over the world who need to transport dead bodies and big tents.'

I had a feeling the three-bike transport system really needed three people. We only had two, which meant a lot of juggling the dead body and propping the bikes up against trees. Finally we managed to get the kangaroo into position.

It wasn't easy, wheeling such a heavy load on a bumpy dirt track, but we stuck at it. Sooner or later we'd have Carla to help us.

If she'd got away from the truck driver.

I didn't want to think about what would have happened if she hadn't, so I changed the subject.

'This is a really clever idea,' I said to Henry. 'It's much easier than carrying or dragging.'

'Whenever possible,' said Henry, 'a scout should be inventive and resourceful.'

'And grateful,' I said. 'Thanks, Henry.'

My phone pinged. It was a text from Carla.

She'd got away.

Henry and I grinned with relief.

Then another message came through, also from Carla. Letting us know she'd hurt her foot and was heading home in a taxi.

Henry and I looked at each other.

'Oh well,' said Henry. 'By the time we get to Carla's place, we'll be experts at the three-bike transport system.'

'And very tired,' I said.

'I don't mind,' said Henry.

'Me neither,' I said.

Being a bit tired was nothing when I thought of the evidence we had.

Evidence that innocent kangaroos were being slaughtered and that the people doing it had probably tried to kill an innocent man.

22

Earless

'Evidence,' I croaked in an exhausted voice to Carla as she dragged me and Henry and the kangaroo along the side of her house.

I understood why she wanted to get us out of sight. It was still dark, but there were lights on in some of the neighbours' houses. Even if the people inside were half asleep and only just out of bed, they'd still probably notice two weary scouts wheeling three bikes and a dead kangaroo.

Carla didn't say anything until she'd helped us get the kangaroo safely past the swimming pool and down some steps into a cellar.

I saw she was limping.

'How's your foot?' I said.

'Few bits of glass,' she said. 'I found most of them.'

'Most of them?' I said, concerned.

'I think there's still a couple in there somewhere,' said Carla. 'They'll work their way out.'

'Did you use disinfectant?' said Henry.

Carla gave him a look. Then she turned to me.

'What exactly do you mean?' she said. 'About the kangaroo being evidence?'

I gave Carla a look. Her neighbours obviously weren't the only ones still half asleep.

'Evidence that your suspects are guilty,' I said. 'That your dad was almost certainly attacked by a kangaroo shooter. It's obvious, isn't it? A person who can knock off innocent kangaroos in cold blood probably wouldn't find it difficult to shoot the author of an annoying book.'

'Even if it was well-written,' said Henry hastily.

Carla sighed.

'Ludo,' she said. 'I told you it's not that simple.'

Henry and I had discussed this on our long plod across Canberra.

We'd decided that what Carla had meant by it being not simple was that we had to be careful making accusations to people's faces when they were carrying high-powered guns.

'It's much simpler now we've got evidence,' I said to Carla. 'When the police see the kangaroo, they'll have to arrest the suspects.'

Carla sighed again.

'The kangaroo shooters aren't the only suspects,' she said. 'There are loads of other suspects. Heaps of them.'

I was dizzy with tiredness, but this made my head feel even more scrambled.

'There can't be,' I said.
'There are,' Carla said.
'So why did you only show us the kangaroo-shooter suspects?' said Henry.
'Come with me,' Carla said.

Carla took us into her dad's office, which luckily was next to the pool so we didn't have to go into the house and risk disturbing her mum or her nan or any armed police.
A computer sat on Mr Moyle's desk.
Carla clicked the mouse.
'This is from my dad's book,' she said. 'These are the other suspects.'
There were hundreds of them.
Photo after photo after photo, all of groups of people. Farmers rounding up sheep. Engineers on building sites in hard hats. Householders putting out the garbage. Horse breeders in fields. Golfers playing golf. Scientists looking into microscopes. Crowds of people demonstrating. And on and on.
Now I was confused.
I glanced at Henry. I could see he was too.
'This is why it isn't simple,' said Carla. 'Everybody has their own personal feelings about kangaroos. Some people want to save them, some people want to get rid of a few, some want to get rid of them all.'
'Why would anybody want to get rid of any kangaroos?' said Henry.
'Lots of reasons,' said Carla. 'Here's a couple.'

She clicked and two other photos appeared on the screen. Two small lizards. The Striped Legless Lizard and the Grassland Earless Dragon.

'Are they suspects too?' said Henry.

Carla shook her head.

'Around here they're dying out,' she said. 'Lots of different reasons for that. Including, scientists think, kangaroos.'

I stared at the two tiny lizards.

'Doesn't seem fair, does it?' said Carla. 'Having big beautiful kangaroos killed to help protect tiny critters with funny names.'

'No,' I said. 'No, it doesn't.'

'Except,' said Carla, 'you've got a funny name, Ludo. And you were tiny once. And somebody protected you.'

I stared at her.

'In my dad's book,' said Carla, 'he isn't saying who's right or who's wrong about the kangaroos. He's just using it as an example. Of how we make everything personal.'

'That's what his book's about?' I said.

'Yes,' said Carla. 'He says it's about our saddest human habit.'

'Not separating bottles and cans from our other garbage?' said Henry.

Carla gave him a look.

'The habit of thinking that what we feel about something is always right,' she said. 'And that everyone who feels differently is totally wrong.'

'Why is that our saddest habit?' said Henry.

'Remember how you felt,' said Carla, 'when you saw the kangaroos being shot?'

I remembered exactly and I could see Henry did just as much.

'Did you hate the people doing the shooting?' said Carla.

'Not hate,' said Henry. 'I just wanted them in jail.'

He thought some more.

'In tiny cells,' he said.

He thought some more.

'With no wi-fi,' he said.

Then he looked sheepish.

'Alright, yes, I hated them.'

I was starting to understand Carla's point. How the stronger we feel about something, the more stubborn and selfish it can make us.

Suddenly I remembered what Mike said about how everything we do is really for ourselves. But he was wrong, so I pushed the thought away.

'Some people,' said Carla to Henry, 'spend their whole lives feeling like you felt. If they don't like what other people are doing, they take it personally. If someone doesn't agree with them, they hate that person. Ask my dad.'

Her face fell. I knew why. We couldn't ask her dad because he was still unconscious.

Is that who the other suspects are?' said Henry. 'People who think your dad doesn't agree with them, and hate him.'

Carla nodded slowly.

She looked sadder than I'd ever seen her look.

'Carla,' I said, 'do you think you'll ever find out who tried to kill your dad?'

She looked at me, her eyes full of tears, and shook her head.

23

Legless

I'd never been so tired and totally exhausted. By the time I finally arrived at our street, I could hardly move the pedals.

I envied Henry, fast asleep in the guest room next to Carla's swimming pool. I even envied the poor dead kangaroo, stretched out in Carla's dad's wine cellar.

Even though I was exhausted, my mind wouldn't stop buzzing. I was thinking about how quickly and easily I'd decided that a kangaroo shooter must have tried to kill Carla's dad. How quickly and easily I'd found someone to blame. How that had made me feel better. And how much I admired Carla for not doing that.

I was thinking about how things shouldn't be always about us. But how they usually are, at least partly. And how Mum had reminded me of that when she died.

I was thinking about how unusual Dad was, to be able to help people without thinking of himself at all. How did he learn to be so unselfish? Was it scouts, or just being married to Mum?

I was thinking all these things as I forced my weary legs to keep pedalling down our street in the overcast morning light.

The one thing I was trying not to think about was Mrs Bayliss. And whether she'd noticed that I'd been missing from my room all night. I was starting to worry that messing my bed up before I left might not be enough.

At least there weren't any messages from her on my phone, even though it was after eight o'clock, which was a good sign.

Sleep in, Mrs B, I said silently. Please sleep in.

I started saying it in rhythm with my pedalling, which must have sort of hypnotised me because I was almost outside our house before I saw who was waiting there for me.

My insides froze.

It was the angry man from the airport. The one who shouted things at Dad. The one whose angry family member chucked the burger.

I wanted to pedal away fast, but my legs just weren't up to it.

'Ludo, mate, good to see you,' said the man. 'Save me ringing the bell.'

I stared at the man, confused.

How did he know my name?

'Excuse me for being a bit rude,' said the man. 'Turning up without an invitation. But I just want to apologise.'

He held out his hand.

Dazed, I shook it.

'I'm Darryn,' said the man. 'Pleased to meet you, Ludo. Saw the stuff about you on TV. What you did on the plane. If I'd known, I promise I would not have said those unkind things. We need more of your sort. So please accept my apologies on behalf of my whole family.'

'Thanks,' I said weakly.

'Just on my way to work,' said Darryn. 'If I could impose for a quick selfie, I'll get out of your hair.'

I leaned my bike against the front fence and stood there while Darryn put his arm round me. I hoped my clothes didn't smell. The three-bike transport system was effective, but sweaty.

Darryn took a few selfies of him and me.

'You're a champ, Ludo,' he said. 'Keep on doing what you do.'

He shook my hand again.

Somehow my dazed and tired brain came up with a thought.

'How do you know where I live?' I asked.

'My brother-in-law drives a Commonwealth car,' said Darryn. 'They know where everyone lives. See you.'

He got into a van, waved through the window, and drove off.

I turned towards the house, half wondering if I was already in bed and dreaming.

Mrs Bayliss was standing at the front door in her dressing gown, looking at me with a puzzled expression. I rather unkindly wished she'd vanish like people do when you're dreaming, so I'd know I was.

She didn't.

'Who was that?' she said.

'Someone I met at the airport,' I said. 'He saw Dad on TV and wanted a selfie with me.'

That was all basically true.

'Come back into the house,' said Mrs Bayliss. 'Where's Henry?'

'He's at Carla's,' I said.

That was true as well.

Mrs B didn't say anything else, so everything seemed to be OK. With a bit of luck, she'd suggest that I go back to bed now for a sleep-in myself.

Then I had another thought.

'Have you heard from Dad?' I said at the front door.

Mrs B's face went very serious.

'Come inside,' she said. 'There's something I have to tell you.'

24

Paulie

Mrs Bayliss told me to sit down at the kitchen bench, but she didn't make me a cup of tea or a plate of sausages or anything.

Just sat down next to me. Which was unusual.

'Have you sent your father a message?' she said.

I shook my head.

'I think you should,' she said.

Which was a bit puzzling.

'I didn't think there was any point,' I said. 'Mike said Dad hasn't got a phone signal on the fundraising boat. And you said Mike left a couple of messages for when Dad does get a signal. Asking him to come back.'

'I still think you should,' said Mrs B.

I had a strange feeling that she was trying to tell me something else. Sometimes, when there are things adults don't want to say, they say other things but they mean the first thing.

A scary thought had been lurking inside me ever since Mrs B's face went serious just now at the front door.

'Has something happened to Dad?' I said.

'No,' said Mrs B. 'I just think he'd like to hear from you when he can.'

'Thanks,' I said to her, very relieved. 'That's kind of you to be concerned about him.'

Mrs Bayliss leaned forward and peered at my head. She plucked something out of my hair and stared at it.

It was a small tuft of fur, grey and soft.

'That's very strange,' said Mrs B. 'This looks like kangaroo fur.'

Now I really did wish Mrs Bayliss had made me a cup of tea or a plate of sausages. So I'd have something to look at so I could keep my eyes away from her.

'Ludo,' she said, 'is there something you should tell me?'

I told her.

There was no point pretending. Mrs B already knew I'd been out all night, I realised that as soon as I saw the way she was looking at me.

A housekeeper with her vast experience could probably spot the difference between a bed that's been slept in and one that's been hand-rumpled just by looking. From outer space, probably.

I decided it was better for her to know exactly

what I'd been doing. Rather than her worrying I'd been at a nightclub or doing graffiti or driving for Uber.

I told her about the kangaroo cull and the three-bike transport system and Mr Moyle's book and Carla's heaps of suspects and the habit we humans have of making everything personal.

Mrs B seemed to already know about a lot of it.

The only thing I didn't tell her about was the dead kangaroo in Mr Moyle's wine cellar. I thought that as a housekeeper, she might find it upsetting from a personal cleaning point of view.

'I'm sorry I deceived you,' I said. 'Specially while you were sleeping.'

'I forgive you, Ludo,' she said. 'But there's something I have to show you.'

She reached over and picked up her iPad.

'Just now before I heard you talking outside,' she said, 'I was watching the news.'

I waited while Mrs B opened a news website and tapped on a segment. She held the screen so we could both see it.

Next to a newsreader at a desk were some words in big letters.

Search For Suspect.

'Police have released details of a suspect,' said the newsreader, 'in the violent attack on retired federal minister Vincent Moyle.'

A photo of a boy appeared on the screen.

A skinny boy holding a kitten.

'Paulie Mitchell Cooper, aged fourteen,' said the newsreader, 'has been on the run from a youth detention centre for several weeks. Members of the public are cautioned not to approach the boy, as he is considered dangerous.'

Mrs B froze the image of the boy on the screen.

My insides were frozen as well.

'Doesn't look particularly dangerous to me,' said Mrs B. 'Or fourteen, come to that. Poor kid looks about nine. I'd say he hasn't had a decent meal for months, if ever.'

I agreed with her.

But I had a feeling this wasn't why Mrs B had shown him to me.

'I'm very glad,' she said quietly, 'you've discovered that some things aren't as simple as they appear, Ludo. That sometimes people choose to see things the way that suits them.'

I looked at her, my tired mind buzzing again.

'What are you thinking?' said Mrs B.

'I don't know,' I said. 'I don't know what to think.'

Then suddenly I did.

'I think the authorities are very lucky,' I said. 'If that boy attacked Mr Moyle, they'll just get blamed for bad security at a youth detention centre. If a kangaroo shooter did it, they'll be blamed for letting armed killers with illegal silencers roam Canberra secretly at night.'

'That's a slightly lurid way of putting it,' said Mrs B. 'But it's probably how some of the media will.

And you're right, a lot of people would prefer that it was young Paulie who did it. Specially MPs who are getting nervous about kangaroos. Now that so many voters are criticising their MPs for letting our national animal be killed.'

We both went silent.

'If the boy didn't do it,' I said after a bit, 'if this is just a mistake, they'll let him go, won't they?'

Mrs Bayliss didn't say anything.

'They have to,' I said. 'All MPs promise to help people and tell the truth. They swear it on the Bible. If there's a mistake, they'll step in and sort it out.'

'Most of them would want to,' said Mrs B. 'But they have to do what their party leaders tell them. And political parties can be very selfish. Most MPs aren't independent like your dad.'

I was feeling weak and dizzy now, and it wasn't anything to do with lack of sleep.

'But they promised,' I said.

'I'm sad to say, Ludo,' said Mrs B, 'it isn't like that. MPs don't have to promise to help people or tell the truth. All they have to promise is to be loyal to the Queen of England.'

I stared at her.

'I can see how disappointed you are by that,' said Mrs B. 'I think a lot of MPs are, when they find out.'

Disappointed? I was more than disappointed. I was outraged.

This just wasn't fair on MPs. They were only human, but when they were tempted to be selfish, they didn't even have a promise to help them put other people first.

Even scouts have that.

I slumped forward onto the kitchen bench.

What hope was there, for Paulie Cooper, or justice, or anything?

Even before I finished asking the question, I knew the answer.

Dad.

'Don't forget to send your dad a message,' said Mrs B.

'I won't,' I said.

I pulled out my phone.

'While you're doing that,' said Mrs B, 'I'll make you some breakfast. Then you must sleep.'

'Thanks,' I said. 'But I haven't got time to sleep. I need to find out the truth about what's going on. So when Dad gets back he can help the other MPs to be fair and honest with Paulie Cooper.'

Mrs B sighed.

'I should probably make you stay here, Ludo,' she said. 'But I'm not going to. I've been doing this job for more than twenty years and I've spent almost all that time not interfering with bad behaviour. Well as of today, I've decided to turn over a new leaf. I'm going to start not interfering with good behaviour.'

25

PM

Mum was a big believer in silver linings.

'That's the thing about dark clouds,' she used to say. 'Silver linings. Not every dark cloud in the world has them, but some do.'

I don't think Mum ever visited Canberra, so she wouldn't have experienced just how bleak the weather can be. But I'm sure she would have been pleased if she'd seen us that day, in a street behind some shops, under a Canberra sky full of dark clouds, finding a silver lining.

It was on the reverse side of a street person's groundsheet.

Polyetheline acetate, it looked like to me. Forty grams per square metre, heat-bonded.

'Back for another good turn, are you?' said the elderly man we'd met a couple of nights earlier.

He smoothed down his groundsheet, which was flapping a bit in the breeze. He was still leaning against the fence and his not-so-elderly friend was still lying down.

'Hello,' I said to them, 'I'm Ludo, and these are my friends Henry and Carla. We're looking for Paulie Cooper.'

'Arthur,' said the man. 'Pleased to meet you.'

'Gavin,' said the other man. 'Likewise.'

We all said hello.

'If you were a few years older,' said Arthur, 'I'd have you pegged for the serious crimes squad, but I'm guessing you're not.'

'We're scouts, remember?' said Henry.

He nodded towards Carla.

'She's not, but she's just as good.'

Carla gave him a look.

'I know who you are,' said Arthur to me. 'Saw you and your dad in the paper. Good on you.'

'Thanks,' I said. 'You probably read about Paulie too. We're trying to find him, to hear his side of the story and make sure he gets treated fairly.'

'That would be a very good turn,' said Arthur.

I knew Carla was itching to say something. That if it turned out Paulie had attacked her father, the fair treatment should include being locked up for a long time.

Henry and I had explained to Carla that if she actually said that to Arthur, we'd probably never find Paulie.

'Can you give us some more clues,' said Henry. 'About where to find him?'

Arthur thought about this.

'Clues,' he said. 'Dunno about that. But I can take you to a bloke who can.'

I would have hugged Arthur if I'd known him better.

'What bloke?' said Carla.

'The PM,' said Arthur.

Arthur insisted on taking us himself, on foot, which meant we had to wheel our bikes very slowly.

He wouldn't say any more about the PM or how the PM could help us.

I could see Carla was doubtful about Arthur. Probably thinking Arthur was suffering a bit of dementia. I'd seen people make that mistake before. Confusing dementia with homelessness.

Poor Carla was still limping a lot, which probably explained her making that mistake. I could imagine how it must be extremely hard to think clearly with bits of glass in your foot.

Arthur just wanted to talk about being a scout.

'I was a scout myself,' he said. 'A Queen's Scout.'

I was impressed. Henry was too. Because not just anybody got to be a Queen's Scout. It was the very top of the scouting climbing wall.

Maybe, I thought, Arthur really does know the Prime Minister.

'Ludo,' said Arthur. 'Personal question. Have you always kept your scout promise?'

I thought about this.

I'd very nearly broken it with Mike, when there was something I needed very badly. I was glad I hadn't. It's why I felt sympathetic to MPs who were tempted. They just needed a bit of help, like Mrs B had given me.

'Yes,' I said to Arthur. 'I have always kept it.'

'Good on you,' said Arthur, looking glum. 'Wish I had. Specially the bit about using resources wisely. Money and love, I haven't used those resources very wisely at all.'

I gave Arthur a sympathetic look.

'Keep the promise as long as you can,' Arthur said to me sternly. 'All of it. Because one day you won't be able to. Happens to everybody. Ah, here we are. The PM.'

I looked around, confused.

It wasn't the Lodge, the big house where the Prime Minister hangs out.

It was a large shop, almost a warehouse.

The sign across the front said The Pet Man.

'Officially he's the Pet Man,' said Arthur. 'But everyone calls him the PM.'

The PM was a grizzled-looking man with a ponytail and orange overalls.

As soon as we stepped into the shop, he ambled over and gave Arthur a hug.

'Good to see you, Arthur,' said the PM.

All around us were long shelves piled with big bags of pet food and kitty litter.

I couldn't see any actual pets.

'This is Ludo,' said Arthur. 'You can trust him. He's a scout.'

'Good to hear,' said the PM. 'But why would I need to trust him?'

'I'll get to that,' said Arthur. He pointed to Henry and Carla. 'He's a scout too. And she's as good as.'

Carla rolled her eyes.

'And you kids,' said Arthur, 'you can trust the PM. He's a top bloke. Gives food to us street folk for our dogs, no charge.'

'Not just dogs,' said the PM. 'Kittens sometimes.'

I wasn't sure if the PM meant that to be a clue, but I decided to gratefully accept it as one.

'We're looking for Paulie Cooper,' I said to the PM. 'We want to make sure he gets treated fairly and justly. Arthur said you could point us in the right direction.'

The PM looked at me. He seemed doubtful.

Arthur spoke up.

'I did say that,' he said to the PM. 'Ludo's dad has just been elected to the Federal Parliament. Independent. You might have seen him in the paper. I reckon young Paulie could use a friend in high places right now.'

The PM thought about this.

'There's been a mistake alright,' he said. 'Paulie wouldn't attack anybody. Feral cats, maybe, when they try to monster his kitten. But I've never known Paulie so much as get into a punch-up. So not only has there been a serious mistake, I'd say there's been a serious miscarriage of justice.'

'I should have mentioned,' said Arthur to me. 'He goes on as much as the other PM.'

'So can you point us in the right direction?' I said to the PM. 'To Paulie?'

'I can do more than that,' said the PM. 'I can point you to the exact spot.'

26

Slug

'I didn't do it,' said Paulie. 'I wasn't even at Mount Costello Reserve that night. I was sleeping near Parliament House.'

He was one of those kids you feel sorry for as soon as you see them.

Mum and me had met quite a few. They looked tough, but also like they did a lot of crying. Sometimes that was an act, but mostly it was real.

Paulie, sitting in the PM's tea room at the back of the shop, on a vinyl chair that seemed too big for him, stroking a straggly kitten on his lap, looked real.

And scared.

I know Mum would have given him a hug.

I reminded myself not to think Paulie was innocent just because I felt sorry for him. This was about him and Carla's dad, not me.

'How old is Fergus?' Carla asked Paulie, stroking the kitten, which was good of her, trying to take his mind off things. But a bit surprising, given her feelings. She must have felt sorry for him too.

'Dunno,' said Paulie. 'PM gave him to me.'

'About two months,' said the PM.

In person, Paulie was even smaller for a 14-year-old than he'd looked in his photo on TV.

Mrs B had been right, he didn't look like he'd had enough to eat when he was little.

I hoped he was making up for it now.

Judging by the finger-bun crumbs on the big plate on the table, it looked like he was trying.

'We haven't got much time,' the PM said to me. 'How quick can your dad get here?'

I explained about the fundraising boat and Dad having no phone signal.

The PM looked like that was really bad news.

'We've left messages,' I said. 'Dad'll be here soon I hope. We just have to keep you hidden, Paulie, while you tell us your side of the story and we check the details for when Dad gets here.'

'You can stay at my place,' said Henry to Paulie. 'We've got really thick curtains.'

'It's too late for that,' said the PM.

We all looked at him. Why was it too late?

'I've called the police,' said the PM. 'They'll be here any minute.'

I stared at the PM, horrified.

So did Carla and Henry.

The PM looked apologetic, but it was Paulie who spoke up.

'We talked about it,' said Paulie. 'And the PM reckoned if I was innocent, which I am, I'd be better off giving myself up. Staying on the run would just make me look guilty.'

'Makes sense to me,' said the PM.

At that moment, from not too far away, we heard a police siren approaching.

Arthur looked nervous.

'Something that makes sense to me,' he said, 'is saying goodbye to you fine people. Me and the police aren't mates. Good luck, Paulie.'

He squeezed Paulie's hand and hurried out.

The siren was very close now.

What should we do? I thought. Run for it with Paulie and try to get him to Henry's place?

I was wondering how we could get him there without being seen by a police helicopter when I realised it was too late.

The siren had stopped outside the shop.

'Be brave, mate,' said the PM to Paulie. 'It'll be alright.'

'Look after Fergus for me,' said Paulie, standing up shakily and handing the kitten to the PM.

'Don't forget your weapon,' said the PM. 'They'll probably let you go when they see that.'

Paulie picked up something from under his chair, something I hadn't noticed. It was a piece of metal shaped like the letter Y with a plastic hand-grip and a loop of black rubber dangling from it.

I realised what it was.

A slingshot.

'And these,' said the PM.

He handed Paulie a small plastic pouch.

I stared at the slingshot. Was this what the police thought had made a life-threatening hole in Mr Moyle? That was crazy.

'Don't worry, Paulie,' I said. 'We'll be collecting evidence and as soon as my dad is back, he'll make sure you get a fair trial.'

If I'd been Paulie, I would have wanted details about how exactly we were going to do that.

But Paulie just muttered, 'Thanks.'

I was glad he didn't ask. I knew Dad and me and the others could help him, I just wasn't sure exactly how we were going to do that yet.

There was something else nagging at me.

Seeing that slingshot was starting to make me feel anxious. I wasn't sure why. I'd never used one or had one used against me.

But my insides weren't feeling good about it. And my brain was starting to ask a question I didn't want it to.

Henry and Carla and I crouched behind a pile of paper sacks of Supabsorb Pet Litter Hygiene Beads.

The PM had told us to stay out of sight.

'Unless,' he said, 'you want the cops to think you're involved in this.'

We could see two burly police officers coming into the shop.

I hoped the Supabsorb Beads didn't absorb sound, because I wanted to hear everything the police officers said.

We could only see Paulie from behind, but from the droop of his thin shoulders I knew what he must be feeling.

I wished I could be there, standing at his side, letting the police officers know that they were doing their jobs and we scouts were doing ours.

'Good decision, PM, making the call,' said one of the officers. 'Saved yourself a harbouring felon charge.'

'I didn't do it for me,' said the PM.

'I didn't do it either,' said Paulie. 'Any of it.'

One of the police officers took the slingshot from him.

'I mean, look at that weapon,' said the PM. 'Are you telling me a thing like that could put a man close to death?'

'Yup,' said the officer. 'I've seen a video of one very similar to this putting a metal slug through a police car door.'

'Oh, come on,' said the PM. 'Paulie just uses it to keep feral cats away from his kitten.'

'We know,' said the officer. 'We've told him to stop more than once. Confiscated a couple of these illegal weapons of assault from him already.'

Paulie's shoulders seemed to droop even more.

I suddenly wished more than ever that Dad hadn't gone on that fundraising trip.

Yes, the money was important because it could be used to help people. But somebody here needed Dad's help even more.

Things weren't looking good for Paulie. Which was exactly when a person most needed a fair trial.

Then, in the pet store, things started looking even worse for him.

Because of what he was suddenly doing.

The one thing a suspect shouldn't do unless he wants to make himself look really, really guilty.

Try to run for it.

27

Me

'Paulie,' yelled the PM.

Paulie got about six steps towards the shop door, slipped on some spilt chook feed and went sprawling.

One of the police officers strode over, picked him up and kept hold of him.

I found it very hard to stay hidden behind the Supabsorb Pet Litter Hygiene Beads. I could tell that Henry and Carla were feeling the same.

Yes, we were concerned about Paulie.

But I was confused. He was in possession of a weapon that could have done the crime. And now he'd just behaved like somebody who had done it.

I struggled to think clearly.

Paulie had said he wasn't at the Mount Costello Reserve on the night of the attack. So before the police could convict him, they'd have to prove he was. Which they couldn't if he wasn't there.

Part of me wanted to stand up and make that point to the police officers in a loud voice.

I didn't.

But I might as well have done, because the police officer holding Paulie had an answer to it.

He bent down and picked up a handful of grey pellets from the floor.

Not chook feed pellets, different ones. They were spilling out of the plastic pouch that Paulie must have dropped when he fell.

The police officer held out his hand for Paulie and the PM to see them.

'Steel-coated lead,' said the officer. 'The victim has a hole in his thoracic cavity. A bullet makes a hole. So does one of these at close range.'

Paulie was looking panicked.

'Except I wasn't there,' he said.

'Strange,' said the police officer. 'Because we found several of these slugs in the clearing right next to the victim.'

Paulie looked like he was falling off a very high climbing wall, which is exactly how I felt too.

'They've got the mongrel,' muttered Carla.

'No,' I said.

I stared in horror at the metal slugs scattered on the shop floor. I remembered where I'd seen them before. On the ground at Paulie's sleeping place near Parliament House. I remembered picking a few of them up so nobody would hurt themselves by treading on them with bare feet.

I remembered putting them into my pocket with the empty cat-food tin.

'What's wrong?' said Carla.

She must have heard the moan of horror that had just come from my throat.

The police officers were leading Paulie out the door. I jumped to my feet, to run after them, to explain. Carla grabbed me and so did Henry.

'It's a fair cop, Ludo,' said Carla. 'We have to let them take him.'

They pushed me back down behind the Hygiene Beads. I didn't need much pushing. I slumped against the sacks.

'You don't understand,' I said. 'It's all my fault.'

I told them about the metal slugs. How I'd forgotten to throw them away when I'd kept the cat-food tin to show Dad when he got back.

'They were still in my pocket when we found your dad, Carla,' I said. 'I pulled my scarf out of my pocket for a compression bandage. I must have accidently pulled the slugs out with it and they must have fallen on the ground next to him.'

Henry and Carla were staring at me, horrified.

I didn't blame them.

'I'll go to the police station,' I said. 'Right now. And make a statement.'

'No,' said Carla.

Her phone rang. She glanced at it. And looked concerned.

'It's my mother,' she said. 'I have to answer it.'

I was still in shock, but I knew how Carla felt. The fear that every call could be the worst possible news. I tried to hear what Carla was saying into the phone, whether it was about her father. But I couldn't because Henry was gripping my arm and speaking to me urgently.

'Ludo,' he said, 'think about it. Your statement wouldn't be enough. It wouldn't. It just wouldn't.'

I didn't know what he was on about.

'It would be the truth,' I said. 'The truth is always enough.'

'Not this time,' said Henry. 'It wouldn't be enough this time.'

I was about to yell at him for being an idiot, but before I could, Carla finished her call. She was looking even more stressed than before.

'I've got to go,' she said. 'My nan went down to the wine cellar to get a bottle of sherry.'

Me and Henry stared at her.

'She found the kangaroo?' said Henry.

Carla nodded.

'Is she OK?' I said.

'She's drinking the sherry,' said Carla. 'I'm sorry, I've got to go.'

'And I've got to go to the police station,' I said.

'No,' said Carla. 'Think about it. If there are MPs who want Paulie to be the attacker so nobody thinks it's a roo shooter, there's a risk they'd make sure your statement was filed away and forgotten. Your word against theirs.'

'I was trying to say that,' said Henry.

'Listen to Henry,' said Carla. 'He's smarter than he looks.'

Henry glowed.

'I'll find MPs who are honest,' I said. 'Who'll stand up for the truth.'

'But which ones are they?' said Carla. 'Right now, we don't know who we can trust. Except for your dad.'

'I was also saying that,' said Henry.

'There's only one way to save Paulie,' said Carla. 'Find out who tried to kill my father. Really strong proof nobody can ignore. More incriminating than just a dead kangaroo, which my nan might already have put out for the council clean-up.'

I looked at Carla and Henry.

It wasn't going to be easy, and I wished they weren't right, but they were.

28

Glass

The Mount Costello Bush Reserve had a fence this time. It was actually police tape, draped across the whole entrance to the reserve, but it was meant to keep people out.

It didn't work with me and Henry.

We looked around to make sure no police were there, then dragged our bikes under the tape and pedalled up the bush road into the reserve.

There was no sign of the kangaroo.

I didn't want to think about what might have happened to her.

Luckily there were no police further up the dirt road either, or in the clearing.

Henry and I parked our bikes and got to work.

Mr Moyle's sleeping bag was gone, and his other things. At first I couldn't find any of the metal slugs, but then I found one. Which made me feel sick again. Evidence of my own carelessness.

'Don't bother looking there,' called Henry. 'We know the police have done that patch. We should be looking where the police might not have bothered.'

Henry was over on the other side of the clearing, scratching in the dust near the drag marks, which were now partly covered with tyre tracks.

I went to another part of the clearing and began searching in some long grass. I didn't know what I was looking for, which made it hard, but suddenly I realised how much I wanted to find something, to make up for what I'd done.

'It's not a competition,' said Henry.

'What have you got?' I said.

We'd been there for ages. Then Henry had given a triumphant yell, so I had too.

'You first,' he said.

I showed him the rock I'd found. I had been studying it and puzzling over it for several minutes. It was the size of a cricket ball, but jagged.

'I think this is blood,' I said, pointing to a dark stain on one side.

Henry peered at the stain.

'Could just be dirt,' he said.

'Look,' I said. 'I think there are tiny dark hairs stuck in the stain. They could be human hairs.'

'Unlikely,' said Henry.

'A scout,' I said sternly, 'remains open-minded at all times.'

'Good point,' said Henry. 'I think I know where

we can get professional forensic advice about hair and probably blood too.'

'That's fantastic,' I said. 'What have you found?'

Henry opened his hand. Lying on his palm were several small fragments of glass.

'Interesting,' I said. 'Could be from a thermos that got broken, or a watch that got shattered, or binoculars that got dropped, or glasses that got trodden on.'

Henry frowned at the fragments of glass as if he was considering all these possibilities.

He looked at me.

'I think they're from a rifle,' he said. 'A high-powered hunting rifle. A broken lens from the scope.'

I peered at the glass. It was possible.

And something else was possible too.

If it turned out that a kangaroo shooter had attacked Carla's dad, people would be even more angry with MPs for letting the cull happen. Angry with all MPs, including Dad.

I pushed the thought away. Dad would never let selfishness get in the way of doing the right thing, and I wasn't going to either.

'How can we find out for sure if this glass is from a gun?' I asked Henry.

'Carla's place,' said Henry.

'Be very quiet,' said Carla as she hurried us into her swimming pool changing room. 'Mum and Nan are very stressed. If they see you, they'll flip. I had to tell them the kangaroo was yours.'

'Just show us the bin,' I said, 'and we'll be gone.'

Carla pointed to a waste bin under the sink.

I tipped the contents onto the floor and carefully hunted through the tissues and nail clippings.

'Yes,' I said.

Two small fragments of bloodstained glass.

'They must have hurt,' I said to Carla.

'Didn't feel them at first,' she said. 'I was so hyped up for the run, I didn't even realise the bloke had busted the gun scope with his camping chair. Didn't feel the mongrels till after I'd lost him.'

'How's your foot now?' I said.

'Getting better,' she said. 'Just one last tiny bit in there somewhere.'

Henry and I studied the pieces of hunting-rifle glass Carla had brought home in her foot. We compared them to the pieces Henry had found at the Mount Costello Bush Reserve.

They were the same.

'Good observing,' I said to Henry.

'Very good,' said Carla.

'Thank you,' said Henry, beaming.

On the way to our next stop, Henry and I bought a drink because a scout has to look after his health and nutrition, and you can't help anybody if you're fainting from dehydration.

While we had our drinks, I wrote a confession

on a piece of paper I'd got from Carla. I confessed about my careless handling of the slingshot slugs. I confessed about making an innocent boy end up in police custody. I confessed about not hiding him at Henry's when I had the chance.

I apologised for all those things, but I didn't make excuses. Mum taught me that.

Then I sent another message to Dad.

I wanted him to know that we had evidence to help him free Paulie when he got back.

I told him about the glass, and about the bloodstained rock that possibly had human hairs on it, and how we were taking it to get professional forensic advice once we'd finished our drink.

I told him where.

That, as it turned out, was a mistake.

29

Rock

Henry's auntie worked in a very professional beauty parlour. I could tell how professional it was from all the technical and scientific equipment they had. Including hair dryers and a microscope.

'This is very interesting,' said Henry's auntie, as she squinted through the microscope at the rock. 'Usually I only get to look at dandruff.'

'Is it blood?' I asked.

'Not sure,' she said. 'Blood's not really my area.'

I looked at Henry.

So much for expert forensic advice.

'She's not really my auntie,' whispered Henry. 'We just call her that.'

'Hmm,' said Henry's auntie thoughtfully. 'There is one process I could try.'

She carefully lifted the rock out from under the microscope, took a tissue from a box, licked the tissue, then rubbed it on the rock.

She studied the tissue.

'Looks a bit like blood,' she said. 'Or chocolate.'

'What about the hairs?' said Henry. 'Are they hairs?'

Henry's auntie put the rock back under the microscope and studied it for a long time.

'Not exactly hairs,' she said.

Henry gave me a look.

A suspicious person might have thought it was an I-told-you-so look, but I chose not to think that.

'More like parts of an eyebrow,' said Henry's auntie. 'Which I suppose are sort of hairs.'

We stood outside the parlour, discussing the rock.

I peered at the half in my hand. Henry's auntie had broken it with a nail file and kept the other half to do further tests.

'I think it must be blood,' I said. 'You probably wouldn't get bits of an eyebrow on a rock without blood. You'd be much less likely to get bits of an eyebrow with chocolate.'

Henry agreed, which was open-minded and showed what a good scout he was.

Plus we'd both licked the rock, and it definitely didn't taste like chocolate.

'Wouldn't it be a breakthrough,' I said, 'if either Mr Moyle or Paulie had a wound from a rock on one of their eyebrows.'

Henry thought about this.

'But they haven't,' he said.

'No,' I said. 'I know.'

It was alright for Henry. He'd had some sleep.

'Oh well,' said Henry kindly. 'Worth mentioning. A good scout explores all possibilities.'

'Thanks,' I said.

Then another possibility hit me. A totally non-sleepy one that really could be a breakthrough.

'Perhaps,' I said, 'it's the attacker who has got the wound. You know, on his or her eyebrow.'

Henry wasn't listening.

He was looking around wildly.

'Our bikes,' he said. 'They've gone.'

He was right. We'd left them parked outside the beauty parlour. They weren't there. Someone must have taken them.

'This sort of crime wouldn't happen,' said Henry bitterly, 'if the police spent less time arresting innocent homeless kids and more time patrolling the streets.'

A car horn beeped nearby. Several times.

We looked around. And saw our bikes poking out of the boot of a parked car. Which, with a sinking tummy, I recognised.

Mike stuck his head out, looking very angry.

'Get in,' he said.

30

Paper

Henry and I both got into the back of the car. Neither of us wanted to sit in the front seat next to Mike.

I wished it was a Commonwealth car, because then there'd be a driver to prevent any violence that might be about to happen. But it was Mike's own car, so he was free to do anything.

'You've been busy boys,' said Mike.

Neither of us replied, though I wanted to ask Mike how he knew.

Government surveillance?

'I think it's time,' said Mike, 'for us to have a little chat.'

Not another one.

It had been bad enough yesterday when he'd tried to bully me into breaking my scout promise. The memory of that sent a jolt of anger through me, and suddenly I didn't feel so scared.

'OK,' I said. 'Am I allowed to go first? I want to tell you about the evidence we've got that proves Paulie Cooper is innocent. And that a kangaroo shooter shot Mr Moyle.'

Next to me on the back seat, Henry wriggled anxiously. I realised I might have exaggerated our evidence, just a bit.

Mike turned in the driver's seat and gave me a long hard look.

I could see he wasn't feeling even a bit scared. Nothing I'd just said had sent a single jolt of fear through any part of him.

'I think,' he said, 'it's time you stopped playing your stupid little games. Which, incidentally, are a complete waste of effort. First rule of life. Nobody listens to little kids.'

'Scouts,' said Henry.

'You think you know what's what?' said Mike to me, ignoring Henry. 'Well, here's some news for you. Here's what your father's really doing on his little trip. He's getting donations.'

'I know that,' I said.

'Donations,' said Mike, 'to help him in his career. To make sure he's elected next time. So he can stay a fat cat.'

I kept quiet.

There was no point arguing with lies.

'Your father,' said Mike, 'only got elected because of what we call the sympathy vote. Because people felt sorry for him. Because your mum carked it.

That won't happen next time. There are national elections next year, and your dad won't get voted in again unless he has some help. I've arranged for him to get that help.'

I still stayed quiet. It wasn't easy after how that rude mongrel spoke about Mum. But I was starting to feel worried.

'I've arranged for your father to get some very big donations,' said Mike. 'To pay for advertising in his next election campaign. In return, he's giving something to me. His loyalty. The government needs him to be on their side. To do what they tell him. To be in their gang. He's agreed to do that in return for my help.'

'No,' I said.

Being independent was the most important thing to Dad. So he could help people whenever he wanted and nobody could tell him he couldn't. Even when he joined the local council, he promised Mum he'd always be an independent.

'This says yes,' said Mike.

He handed me a piece of paper.

I read it.

A letter from Dad, agreeing to take direction and instruction from the government.

To do what they tell him.

Signed by Dad, with his signature.

A scout never gives up, that's what Henry always said. Well, he was wrong. I was a scout, and that was the moment I gave up.

'So you see,' said Mike, 'if by some chance your little scouting games do end up embarrassing and annoying the government, they'll be harming your father much, much more.'

I'd always felt ill in the back of cars, but never this ill, and we weren't even moving.

'OK,' said Mike. 'Hand them over. The glass, the rock, and the paper.'

How did he know? How did he know about the glass and the rock? Had he been spying on us with a satellite or something?

Henry tried to open the car door.

It was locked.

On the way back to the house, I rang Dad. Just in case he was on dry land.

Mike couldn't stop me, he was driving.

'How could you?' I wanted to say to Dad. 'Everything you've done since arriving in Canberra has just been for yourself.'

I didn't get to say it, though.

In my earpiece, the call just rang and rang.

Then I realised I could hear exactly the same ringing in Mike's briefcase which was next to him on the front seat.

'Oh,' said Mike, 'didn't I mention? Your father forgot his phone in the rush to the airport.'

As if.

Dad had never forgotten his phone in his life.

Mike must have done something. Swapped the

SIM or something. So that no messages got through to Dad. In case I found out what he was really doing on the boat and made him feel guilty.

Which I would have done.

Instead, all I could do was sit in the back of the car feeling like every piece of Henry's broken glass was in my guts.

Dad had lied to me.

Even worse, he'd broken his promise to Mum.

31

Lyle

When we got back to the house, there were people in the street out the front.

Taking selfies.

Mike swore.

'This is because of that cretin from the airport,' he said to me. 'That stupid fan of yours, the one you did the selfie shoot with outside the house. He posted his snaps on Facebook, so now the whole world knows where you live.'

As we drove into the garage, the people out the front peered into the car. They started waving at me and clapping.

'Don't get too full of yourself,' Mike said to me. 'They're just dumb mutts who think politics should be fair and honest. And politicians should fly cattle class. Hilarious. Give any one of them a dollop of power and they'd be doing dirty deals in a business class seat in a blink.'

I didn't say anything. No point. Henry had tried when we dropped him at his place.

'I just want to say,' he'd said to Mike, 'that I don't blame you for being how you are. If your parents had taken you to scouts, you'd be very different.'

Mike had smirked.

And Mike was right. Scouts was no guarantee.

Dad's parents took him to scouts, and look how he turned out.

'Wave goodbye to your fans,' Mike said to me now. 'They'll be in a police van soon. And you get into the house and stay there.'

Inside the house, Mrs B was at the window, peering out at Mike waving his arms in the street.

'Ludo,' she said, 'we've got a situation.'

'It's OK,' I said miserably. 'They're just fans.'

'I don't mean out there,' said Mrs B.

She signalled to me to follow her up the stairs, ignoring my enquiring look. I followed her up.

'By the way,' said Mrs B over her shoulder. 'Did you send your dad a message?'

'Two,' I said quietly. 'He didn't get them.'

I didn't go into details. I was very tired. All I wanted to do was throw myself onto my bed and close my eyes and not think about anything.

Specially not about how Mike was right.

How the whole country, probably, was run by people who only cared about themselves.

People who were elected to help with things.

Schools. Hospitals. Droughts. Wars. Jobs. Kids in pain. Animals in pain. But if they were like Mike or Dad, they only did things to help themselves.

I wished Mum was there, so she could help me feel better.

Then I realised what I was doing, which made me feel even worse.

Mike was right about me too. I was just using Mum to help myself. I was like him and Dad.

At the top of the stairs, Mrs B turned to me.

'I'm not surprised your dad didn't get your messages,' she said. 'After you left this morning I realised that a certain person has probably been making sure of that. So I took the liberty of asking someone I know to get a message through. And if possible to give your dad a lift back.'

I stared at her.

'A lift?' I said. 'From the middle of the ocean?'

'My friend has access to helicopters,' said Mrs B. 'And submarines.'

If anyone else said that, you'd think they were joking. But this was Mrs B. So I just kept staring at her in amazement. And making a note to suggest to Henry that an even better job than MP might be housekeeper.

'First, there's something more urgent we have to attend to,' said Mrs B. 'We have a visitor, who arrived about half an hour ago.'

Mrs B opened my bedroom door.

We went in and I looked around, puzzled.

There was nobody there.

Mrs B went over and opened the door to the walk-in wardrobe.

'Ludo,' she said, 'this is Mr Flanagan.'

Sitting on the floor of the wardrobe, leaning against my suitcase, was a tall skinny weatherbeaten man in tight jeans and battered cowboy boots. He was sipping a cup of tea and eating a cupcake.

On his head, over one eyebrow, was a bandage.

'Hello,' I said, stunned.

'G'day,' said the man.

'Mr Flanagan shot Carla's dad,' said Mrs B.

The man gave her a hurt look.

'That's a bit brutally frank,' he said.

'It was an accident,' said Mrs B.

'Thank you,' said the man.

'Mr Flanagan hasn't known where to turn,' said Mrs B. 'He's fearful that because he was hired in secret, the authorities will try to hush things up. But he's tormented by the thought of an innocent boy unjustly dragged through the –'

'Can I speak?' said the man.

'Sorry,' said Mrs B.

'The name's Lyle,' said the man to me.

He stood up and came out of the wardrobe, holding out his hand.

'Best if you stay in there,' said Mrs B, glancing nervously over her shoulder. 'I may need to close that door at any time.'

Lyle stepped back into the wardrobe and sat down again.

I stopped being frozen with surprise and went in and sat down next to him.

'Hello,' I said. 'I'm Ludo.'

We shook hands. I tried not to show him how totally gobsmacked I was feeling.

'Mrs Bayliss is right,' said Lyle. 'The thought of that kid, wherever they've put him . . .'

His words choked up and for a few moments he couldn't speak. From the anguished look on his face, I had the feeling he knew what Paulie was going through.

'Either way, it's not good,' said Lyle. 'If the authorities hush it up, the kid cops it. Or else they blame me for the whole deal and I'm walloped for attempted murder.'

'That's why he's come to us,' said Mrs B.

'I need someone high up,' said Lyle. 'Someone decent and honest who can get my confession out there in a fair and just way. I couldn't think who. Then I remembered seeing your dad on TV.'

'He's on his way here now,' said Mrs B. 'I hope.'

I could see Lyle was hoping that too.

But would it help him, given the sort of person Dad had turned into?

That was up to Dad.

'Lyle,' I said. 'While we're waiting, can I ask you a question?'

Lyle thought about this.

'If it's not too brutally frank,' he said.

I hoped it wasn't. I asked it anyway.

'How did you shoot Mr Moyle by accident?'

Lyle rubbed his hand over his face. For a second I thought he wasn't going to answer. But he did.

'Mrs Bayliss tells me you know about the cull,' said Lyle.

I nodded. I must have been looking sad, about the cull and about Dad, because Lyle glanced at my face and then looked away.

'I know how people feel,' he muttered. 'But I've got kids, and one of them with medical bills. What can I do? It's my job.'

'We're not judging you,' said Mrs B softly.

'God didn't give me much,' said Lyle. 'But he gave me the eye to hit anything I point a firearm at. No misses, no damage. Not ever. Until a couple of weeks ago.'

His shoulders sagged and he took another sip of tea. Everything that Lyle was doing, including swallowing, looked painful. I felt sorry for him, but I didn't want him to stop.

'I was part of a contracted shooting team,' he said. 'We were doing a mob in Mount Costello Bush Reserve. One of the other blokes took down a joey at foot. The mother was mine. I dunno what it was, tiredness, worry, getting old, but I missed. She scarpered.'

Lyle raised his teacup to his lips.

A painful gulp.

'Kept me awake every night,' he said. 'Thinking of her without her son. I couldn't carry on if that happened to me. Then I heard there was a solo female, coming down out of Costello Reserve each night. All on her own. Going into people's front yards. Just standing. Looking into the houses. Locals hated it, you can imagine, specially the families with kids.'

He paused again.

'I knew it was her,' he said. 'And I owed it to her. To finish the job.'

My heart was going fast and my mouth was dry.

I felt Mrs B's hand on my shoulder and I knew she was asking me not to say anything.

I stayed silent. Lyle was watching me.

'I know,' he said. 'But that's what I felt.'

'Go on,' said Mrs Bayliss gently.

Lyle took another breath.

'Monday night,' he said, 'I finally had her in my sights. Up in the clearing. I was about to take the shot when this homeless bloke, that's what I assumed he was when I got a look at him afterwards, comes running at me out of nowhere, yelling. He chucks a rock or something. It slams into the gun, then riccochets up and hits me in the head. The gun has discharged. Safety's off, there was nothing I could do. Bloke's on the ground. I checked his vitals. No good. As far as I could tell, he was gone.'

Lyle lifted his teacup, but it was empty.

He took a wobbly breath and carried on.

'I panicked. All I could think of was how my family would cope if I was inside. But I couldn't just leave the poor blighter there, out in the open. So I dragged him over and put him on his sleeping bag. I should have done more, I know. I was a mess. Couldn't think straight. Got out of there.'

Lyle put his head in his hands, his whole body trembling.

'Some more tea?' said Mrs B to him softly.

I wished Dad was here.

Now.

Right now.

'Lyle,' I said to him in a shaky voice. 'I think it's going to be OK. We've got evidence that backs up your story. Broken glass from your rifle. And a rock with some of your eyebrow on it.'

'Actually,' said a voice. 'Some of that evidence might have been lost.'

Standing in the bedroom doorway was Mike.

Mrs B jumped up to close the wardrobe door, then realised it was too late.

'I'm sorry,' she said to Lyle.

'Close it if you like,' said Mike. 'I've heard enough. He's perfect. Rogue shooter, completely unauthorised to be there that night. We'll throw the book at him. It's a law-and-order win-win for all concerned.'

Mrs B gave Mike a long look that would have killed a normal person.

'You,' she said, 'are a disgusting excuse for a human being.'

'And you,' said Mike, 'are fired. And may well be prosecuted for obstructing the course of justice.'

Suddenly I could feel Mum in the room.

And I knew she wasn't there just for me.

'Scouting lesson number one,' I said to Mike in the loudest voice I could. 'You reckon people don't listen to kids. Well, let's put it to the test.'

Mike's eyes flared angrily.

I felt a stab of fear, but ignored it.

'There are thousands of scouts in Australia,' I said, 'and millions in the world. Scouts trust each other, so they'll believe me when I tell them about you. And show them the piece of rock you didn't get. And the piece of glass. They'll probably tell their mums and dads about you trying to destroy vital evidence. They'll probably tell their teachers too, and their friends and their scout leaders and their neighbours and their pets.'

Mike took several steps towards me. He only stopped when Mrs B stood at my side.

'Do you really want to do that?' he said to me.

'Yes,' I said to him.

But suddenly I wasn't sure if I did.

'The question you have to ask yourself,' said Mike, 'is am I with my dad or am I against him? Me, I'm with your dad, Ludovic. Because my job is to protect him and I would have thought that was your job too.'

Mrs B squeezed my hand.

'It's not as simple as that,' I said to Mike.

I wondered if anybody, even Mrs B, knew how complicated it was.

Compared to this, my life had been simple. Terrible and painful sometimes, but simple.

This was the hardest choice I'd ever had to make.

If I told the truth, Dad's career would be wrecked. If I didn't, an innocent kid would suffer and the liars would triumph.

'In this game,' said Mike, 'it's very, very simple. You're either with us or you're against us.'

'Oh dear,' said another voice. 'That sounds dramatic. I hope the answer is, with us.'

We all looked over to the doorway.

It was Dad.

32

Dad

'Tell me everything,' said Dad.

I hesitated.

Dad was sitting next to me on the lounge in the living room. Mike was sitting opposite, not saying anything, his eyes burning into me.

His eyes hadn't left me in the bedroom either, not during all the time Dad was hugging me. During all those seconds, Mike looked like he was watching something he hadn't experienced himself very much at all.

If ever.

I hadn't ever experienced a hug exactly like that before either. A hug from Dad that didn't feel right. One that felt like he was somebody else.

A person capable of doing all the things he'd done since I'd last seen him.

All the things I'd discovered.

A selfish person.

'Everything,' said Dad softly. 'Tell me the lot.'

I could hear Lyle and Mrs B talking quietly in the kitchen. For a second I wished she was in here with me. But she wasn't.

It was just me and Dad.

I told him everything.

When I'd finished, Dad didn't speak for a long time.

Just sat staring at the carpet.

It must have been hard for him to hear it all. Specially the details of me finding Mr Moyle and the blood and the dead kangaroos and the number of times I went off the bike paths.

And I could see how painful it was for him to read my written confession about how I'd nearly caused an innocent boy to go to jail.

Even so, he read it about six times.

It must also have been extremely difficult for him to hear some of the other things. For example, how it looked like there were MPs in Canberra who might be tempted to let a fourteen-year-old boy suffer injustice because it would make things better for them at work.

And how I was worried that he might have started turning into one of those MPs.

Dad cleared his throat.

'Thank you for telling me all that, Ludo,' he said. 'You've been brave and you've been honest and you've stood up for what you believe in and I'm proud of you. But I think the excitement of all those new experiences, and the stress of it all, might have made your imagination a bit fevered.'

I closed my eyes.

This was exactly what I didn't want to hear.

Dad trying to make excuses.

'Think about it, Ludo,' said Dad. 'OK, we're all human and sometimes we're all tempted to try and make things a bit easier. But do you really think it's likely, or even possible, that elected representatives would be as ruthlessly selfish as you're suggesting? I just think you've got that wrong.'

That was when I knew I'd lost my dad.

Or would have done if Mike hadn't spoken up.

'Actually,' he said to Dad, 'the kid's got it dead right. That's exactly what some of them are capable of. Not many of them, but more than anybody would imagine in their worst nightmares. Welcome to Canberra.'

Dad looked at him.

On Dad's face was an expression I hadn't seen since Mum died.

'Of course,' said Mike, 'nobody ever admits it. Or even talks about it. Which is why it's very good you're back, Garth. Sometimes it takes a dad to make a kid shut up.'

All the way up the stairs, as I slowly followed Dad, I couldn't stop seeing the expression on Mike's face when Dad said he wanted to talk to me alone.

Triumph.

Dad led me into the bedroom and closed the door behind us.

He sat on the bed and looked up at me.

'Ludo,' he said, and then stopped, and I could see he was struggling.

I tried to imagine what it would be like, to tell your son you'd dumped everything that made us a family.

Everything Mum had given us.

Suddenly I didn't want Dad to have to say it.

I didn't want to have to hear it.

But before I could let him know that, before I could ask him to spare us both the pain, Dad started speaking again.

'Ludo,' he said. 'I am so sorry.'

And then he started to cry.

33

Mum

Mrs Bayliss reckoned Dad's press conference will go down in the history of Canberra as one of the most unusual press conferences ever.

And one of the most emotional.

Actually, the emotion started in the foyer of Parliament House even before Dad went up onto the podium.

The emotion belonged to Mike.

It was mostly anger, with a bit of a tantrum thrown in.

'You're finished,' Mike screeched at Dad. 'Dead in the water. A one-shot wonder.'

Dad's reply to Mike was much less emotional.

'You're fired,' he said.

There were lots of other emotions in the Parliament House foyer that day.

Such as when Henry and Carla came running in.

I'd started to worry they were going to be late, or maybe that they'd even miss the press conference completely. Then I'd started to worry about why that might be.

A call from the hospital?

Terrible news?

As Carla and Henry hurried towards me, I saw that Carla's eyes were as red as they'd been when I first met her in the police centre.

My insides sagged.

Until Carla gave a huge tearful grin.

'He's awake,' she said. 'He's going to be OK.'

Not many of the other emotions that day were as loud as Carla and me and Henry whooping and hugging each other and not caring how many people in the Parliament House foyer were staring.

'I told him about you, Ludo,' Carla said. 'He wants to meet you and Henry to say thank you.'

'And Wattle Patrol,' I said.

Carla turned to the people watching us.

'Scouts,' she yelled, pointing at me and Henry. 'Heroes.'

It was nice of her, but a bit embarrassing.

Most people would also have felt something, I'm pretty sure, when they looked at the big Australian coat of arms on the wall behind the podium.

A quiet feeling, perhaps a puzzled one, but still worth having.

I know I felt it. And Henry and Carla did too, when we'd all calmed down.

The familiar emu and kangaroo, standing at the centre of our national crest, just like we see in our schools and scout halls and on our coins and the uniforms of our soldiers.

But there was something different about this crest. At the base, looking up at all the people, very proud to be Aussies too, were a couple of tiny cardboard cutouts.

A Striped Legless Lizard and a Grassland Earless Dragon.

Some of the things Dad said at that press conference couldn't have been easy.

But he said them anyway.

How for a while he'd forgotten why he'd come to Canberra.

How ashamed he was of that.

And how grateful he was to the people who'd helped him remember.

Including the man sitting next to him, Lyle Flanagan. A man who'd made some mistakes and was honest enough to admit it. A man who was prepared to face the consequences of his actions. A man who deserved to have a fair hearing and who simply hoped for justice – for himself, and his family, and an innocent kid called Paulie Cooper.

Which, thanks to Dad, and Mr Moyle, is what they got.

Dad announced one more thing that day. He told the media that his first project as the newest independent Member of Parliament would be an investigation, and he asked the media to help.

He told them he'd be looking at how the police had handled Mr Moyle's case. Whether anybody, MPs or public servants or anybody else, had put pressure on the police to stop them being truthful and honest.

Dad and I had agreed that if that had happened, it wasn't fair on the police and they deserved some help with it.

Dad didn't mention me at the press conference. We'd agreed I'd had more than enough publicity for an eleven-year-old.

But he looked at me a lot.

I could tell that the conversation we'd had the night before was helping.

Specially the part about Mum. How she would definitely agree that it's totally worth spending a year helping as many people as you can, even if it's your only year. Much better than spending that year trying to get more years in the job, which you'd probably then spend trying to get more years after that. And so on.

I'd reminded Dad of what Mum said once.

'None of us know how long we've got, so we shouldn't put it off. We should try to make a difference now.'

Dad and I agreed that Mum hadn't put it off.

Ever.

Which had got Dad crying again.

And I'd happily joined him.

Mrs B also reckoned that Dad's official swearing-in ceremony will go down in Canberra history as one of the most amazing things ever to happen in Federal Parliament.

And yes, one of the most emotional.

I'll never forget Dad standing there in front of all the other Members of Parliament, one hand on the book, the other raised.

A parliamentary officer said the first few official words that Dad was meant to repeat.

But instead of repeating them, Dad took a deep breath, then said something else.

'I beg leave of the house,' he said, 'to vary the form of my oath.'

Some of the MPs looked a bit surprised.

I probably did too.

Dad didn't wait for permission.

'On my honour,' he said, his voice loud and strong, glancing over at me, 'I promise to do my best. To be true to my spiritual beliefs. To contribute to my community and to our world. And to help other people.'

In the public gallery, Henry and I and the other members of Wattle Patrol looked at each other with delighted amazement.

Carla looked puzzled.

'It's the scout promise,' said Henry. 'He's saying the scout promise.'

Carla's grin was as big as ours.

And Dad didn't stop there, even though a lot of MPs were looking surprised now, and some a bit stunned.

He said all of it.

'I promise to be respectful,' he said. 'To be friendly and considerate. To care for others and the environment. I promise to do what is right. To be trustworthy, honest and fair. To use resources wisely. I promise to believe in myself. To learn from my experiences. And to face challenges with courage.'

When he finished, I waited for the MPs to cheer and applaud.

They didn't.

A few clapped. A couple dabbed their eyes. But most of them stayed silent.

Some, maybe, were feeling confused about why anyone would want to make a promise that would be so hard to keep.

Others, perhaps, stayed silent because Dad had just helped them remember why they came to Canberra in the first place, and had made them think about how it had been going since.

I wasn't silent. Nor were Henry and Carla and the rest of Wattle Patrol.

We cheered and applauded for a long time.

Right up until some officials asked us to stop.

Dad heard us cheering. He looked up at me, and I knew he was thinking the same thing I was.

Mum was right when she said that two out of three is still a family.

But that day, that historic day, all three of us were there in the Parliament of Australia, and yes we were there for ourselves, but mostly we were there for each other.

Dear Reader

It's not just Members of Parliament who need help and encouragement. Authors do too.

I was helped and encouraged in the writing of this book by a number of kind people, and I'd like to give them a big vote of thanks.

For enriching my visits to Canberra with insights into the politics, environment, social customs, history and bike paths of the place, my deepest gratitude to Alex Sloan, Rob and Zoe Thornton, Karen Viggers, David Lindenmayer, Karen Middleton, Caroline Greenway, Tony O'Brien, Carmel McGregor and Paul Cowan.

For letting me borrow his name, even though he didn't know about it at the time, thank you to my friend Ludo.

As always, my colleagues and friends at Penguin Random House made the journey of this book a joy. They unfailingly supported everything I elected to do, including changing the title five times. Warmest thanks to Laura Harris, Julie Burland, Heather Curdie, Tony Palmer, Tina Gumnior, Kristin Gill, Deb van Tol, Dot Tonkin and her marketing team, Angela Duke and her sales team, and everyone else who helped get this book made, distributed and read.

For reading early drafts of the manuscript and giving it the benefit of their deep understanding of children's stories, thank you to my dear friends Sarah Hughes and Anna Fienberg.

And heartfelt appreciation beyond words to my partner, Pam Easton, who listened patiently and with love to me reading the entire book out loud several times. Her thoughts and feelings helped and encouraged me like nothing else.

While I was preparing to write this book, my mother died. You may have spotted a mother's love in this story, and a mother's grace, integrity, kindness and unwavering sense of fair play. Ludo's mother is a made-up character, but if you knew my mother, you'd know where these parts of the story came from. Thanks Mum.

Morris Gleitzman